MiAMI

Hot & Cool

MIAMI

CLARKSON N. POTTER, INC.
PUBLISHERS
New York

Text by
LAURA CERWINSKE

Photographs by
STEVEN BROOKE

Design by
ALEXANDER ISLEY
DESIGN

Hot & Cool

ACKNOWLEDGMENTS

We wish to express our thanks to Debra Lynn Yates;
Mimi Ferre; Susan Rothchild; Marlene Weiss;
Patrick Hamilton; Patricia Fisher; Thorn Grafton;
James Watson; and Nina Woessner of
Fairchild Tropical Garden for their kind help.

Published by Clarkson N. Potter, Inc., distributed by Crown Publishers, Inc.,
201 East 50th Street, New York, New York 10022

CLARKSON N. POTTER, POTTER and colophon are trademarks of
Clarkson N. Potter, Inc.

Manufactured in Japan

LIBRARY OF CONGRESS CATALOGING-IN-PUBLICATION DATA
Cerwinske, Laura.
Miami Hot and Cool/Text by Laura Cerwinske;
photographs by Steven Brooke.—1st ed. p.   cm.
1. Architecture—Florida—Miami.   2. Architecture, Tropical—Florida—Miami.
3. Gardens—Florida—Miami.   4. Miami (Fla.)—Buildings, structures, etc.
5. Miami (Fla.)—Social life and customs.
I. Brooke, Steven.   II. Title.
NA735.M4C47   1990   728'.09759'381—dc20   90-6713
CIP
ISBN 0-517-57431-4

10 9 8 7 6 5 4 3 2 1

First Edition

For Jona, who loves Miami as much as I do.
L.C.

For Suzanne, Molly, and Nat
and for
Dennis, Shu, Jeannie, Valerie, and Mark.
S.B.

MEDITERRANEAN

style

33

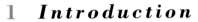

conte

BUNGALOW

style

67

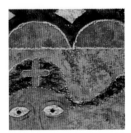

DECO & MODERN

style

103

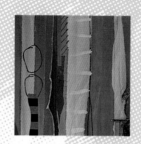

n t s

*g*ARDEN

design

173

miami is a city of sensations:

pounding rains and searing heat; bare feet on cool terrazzo, in warm garden earth, on hot sand; skin salty from the ocean and sweaty from midday sun; summer nights redolent with jasmine, spring evenings perfumed with gardenias, late winter air infused with the scent of orange, grapefruit, and lime blossoms; and steamy afternoons— breezeless, breathless, and tinged with the aroma of pine needles in a smoldering soil.

Miami is the exotic mixed with the suburban. It is contented dogs wallowing in cool dirt or in plastic wading pools. It is cats dozing in oak branches or poising for the hunt of a legion of lizards crawling across patio screens. It is the sudden squawk of parrots flying overhead and the unexpected sight of long-legged egrets and broad-winged anhingas diving for fish

1

from the banks of residential waterways. It is exaggerated shapes and intense growth. It is ripe avocados and bananas hanging from heavily laden trees. It is brilliant glare and rapid decomposition. Yet it is also winter air as delicate as silk. For as brazen as Miami is, it is also elusive, romantic, and exotic.

Other cities may have mountain ranges or great vistas to dramatize their settings, but in Miami it is the flatness of the terrain that affords the city its uninterrupted and continually magical periphery. My mother, who moved to Miami Beach from New York City in 1932, has never forgotten her  first view of the great expanses of yellow sand and the broad, open horizon. She recollects, too, the pleasures of man-made Miami—the anticipation of seeing each season's new buildings and the exhilaration of the town's social atmosphere. My father, an animator with the Fleischer Studios (makers of the Popeye and Betty Boop cartoons), which had moved its facilities from Times Square to Miami in 1938,

remembers Miami Beach—where he met my mother—as a luminous place. He recalls Washington Avenue aglow in neon, the statue of Henry Flagler (the visionary who brought the railroad to Miami in 1896) illuminated at night, and the evanescent play of sunlight on the rippling waters of Biscayne Bay.

The Miami I grew up in, the Miami of the 1950s, was a quiet, seasonally populated town scarcely related to the busy metropolis of today. My neighborhood, around SW 25th Street and 62nd Avenue, was considered a residential frontier; 25th Street became a dirt road beyond the corner where I lived with my mother, father, and brother in a small house built soon after World War II. Although the house was architecturally undistinguished, two towering poinciana trees that canopied the front yard made the setting romantic in my eyes. Every June vivid orange blossoms began to blanket the grass, turning our lawn into a paintbox of green and orange and dappled sunlight. A jalousied porch—a Florida room—built by my father at the side of the house made a cool, shaded, relaxing family room. The porch looked out on a wooded lot that not only gave us privacy, but provided my brother and me, and our friends on the block, a wonderful place to play. When not peppering a baseball around someone's yard, I could always be found in the woods, up a tree, imagining myself as my idol, Sheena of the Jungle.

Across the street from us and the woods, in the middle of a lawn the size of six lots, stood a house made of coral rock that, to my unworldly eyes, seemed a mansion. The lawns, mowed with precise regularity, were ornamented with a goldfish pond and a brilliant green reflecting globe on a stone pedestal. Gardenia bushes and firecracker ferns bordered the house, and to one side of it grew a grove of fruit trees—avocados, mangoes, grapefruit, and Key limes. Between two of these trees was strung a hammock so privately and elegantly situated

that I thought of it as a swinging chaise longue. The property also included a detached garage in which the owners, a retired couple, kept their mint-condition 1951 Cadillac and, curiously, a huge, elaborate electric train set.

I was invited to visit inside the house only a few times, but the considered effect of its rooms has never left me. A sun porch, paved with mosaic tile and furnished with a glass-topped wrought-iron table and canvas-upholstered rattan chairs, was enclosed on three sides with jalousied windows that looked out on the lawns and fruit trees. The kitchen, almost as small as a passageway, was concise and efficient but implied that life went on mostly beyond its walls. The living room had hardwood floors covered with Oriental carpets, and the bedrooms, all located on corners, were well ventilated, with light modulated by wooden venetian blinds. Although this was in the days before universal air-conditioning, I remember that the house always felt cool and serene.

Next door to this "estate" sat another house whose plan equally influenced my sense of subtropical living. It had been designed by early Miami architect Dean Parmalee for his daughter, Dottie Hart, and her family, and my days in the Harts' home were many. Its walls and ceilings were built of Dade County pine. Rightly or wrongly, it always seemed to me that those pine walls made the house smell good and feel cozy (even though it was quite open). Parmalee had given the living room a tall cathedral ceiling and paved the floors with Cuban tiles. Fold-back doors at the back of the house opened onto a screened-in porch (which eventually overlooked a swimming pool) and at the front of the house onto a lawn, entirely cross-ventilating the living room. An attic fan sucked hot air up and kept cool air circulating throughout.

Today, although the Harts still live on 25th Street, the next-door estate is gone, long ago subdivided into four lots, where four blocky contemporary houses now stand. Not only is the street beyond the corner of our old home paved, but the outreaches of suburban Miami now extend more than two hundred blocks farther to the south and west.

Despite the many years I lived in Miami, and no matter how frequently I return, I am always startled by its constant change. So must be my mother, who witnessed the city's evolution from the small town of her youth—a busy, close-knit community of transplanted New Yorkers living in modest apartments around downtown Flagler Street—to the quiet suburbia of mine. And so, I expect, will be my son when he faces the contrasts between the sun-soaked city of his childhood and the one he'll find at the end of this century. For Miami, a city with virtually no community history before the advent of the railroad, has ceaselessly transformed itself, growing from a backwoods frontier to a land speculator's jackpot to an international banking center and refugee mecca, all in a scant one hundred years.

Miami's earliest settlement occurred at the mouth of the Miami River in 1849 when the army built an outpost, Fort Dallas, as a fortress against hostile Seminole Indians. Later, in the 1870s, the Brickell family established the area's first inn and trading post, where they bartered with the Miccosukee Indians who traveled up and down the river, hunting and fishing between the Everglades and Biscayne Bay. In 1895 Julia Tuttle purchased a substantial part of what is now the city of Miami and established a joint venture with Henry Flagler, giving him half her property in exchange for building the  railroad and developing sections of the city. Subsequently, hotels and inns sprang up to serve the blossoming tourist trade, and facilities to provide for the railroad workers helped further the forces of urbanization.

The complex of energies that becomes, over time, the personality of a city did not fully develop in Miami until the 1960s. Unlike other, older American cities with dense pedestrian nexuses, Miami experienced its boom after the advent of the car, and its population—largely of tourists—was transient. "Urbanization begins with the desire to live in an active, diverse and generally intense social community," Miami architect Bernard Zyscovich explains. This social and cultural density did not manifest itself in Miami (with the exception of Miami Beach and Coconut Grove) until hundreds of thousands of Cubans fleeing Fidel Castro's government took up residence in the downtown neighborhood that has since become known as Little Havana.

This Cuban influx led to a cultural phenomenon unique in American history: Unlike America at large, which became a nation of immigrants over the course of centuries, Miami became a city of immigrants overnight. As a former Miami mayor, Maurice Ferre, has pointed out, "Never before has an American city of this size changed the character of its population so radically in one generation. In fact, not only has the process of assimilating other immigrants always been slower in United States history, but never before has it been as overwhelming." Within twenty-five years, Miami's population of Cubans and other Hispanics rose from a negligible proportion to 44 percent—and it is projected to exceed 50 percent of the total population before the year 2000.

Furthermore, as Ferre has noted, most immigrants plant the seeds of their old culture in their new home and spend generations nurturing the new growth to fruition, but the Cubans brought a full-blown culture to Miami. "Not just the seeds, but the whole  forest—trees, shrubs, fauna, birds, a whole society complete with nearly all the elements of their previous culture. Cubans living in Miami can feel very much at home both physically and spiritually, for they have their own radio, television, newspapers, social clubs, insurance companies, banks, and funeral homes —everything required to travel from birth to death as a Cuban." As the number of exiles from Nicaragua, Colombia, Haiti, and other Latin American countries continues to grow, Miami and its surrounding region becomes a center of enormous cultural diversity.

Miami, alternately shameless and discreet, is a city of paradoxes. Its climate fosters openness while its energy code calls for enclosure. Its natives seek a sense of history while its immigrants quest for a future. Founded on real estate fantasies, it is contending with many of today's harshest urban and social realities.

What remains *unchanged* about Miami, regardless of its increasing traffic, relentless suburbanization and growing assortment of populations, is the physical, spiritual, and visual nourishment of living in a light-filled, botanically varied environment. In fact, bringing the outside in is the very key to the region's successful interior design. Whether a house is tropically adapted Mediterranean-style, neoclassical, or contemporary, its windows look out onto views of big palms, broad leaves, and lots of sky. And those views inevitably affect what is done inside. In Miami, hard floors, cool surfaces, and furniture that doesn't obstruct the flow of air make sense indoors. Outdoors, the environment calls for garden furniture that doesn't rot and patios that resist mildew.

A number of Miami architects, such as Andres Duany and Elizabeth Plater-Zyberk, have focused their thinking about local design around the way southern Florida's climate, culture, building techniques, and use of light have been handled historically. Duany and Plater-Zyberk have looked hard at regional traditions, including the  Greek Revival architecture of the south with its temple-style plantations, mansions, and civic buildings. They conclude that the porches of vernacular architecture, the arcades of Mediterranean-style buildings, low-pitched roofs that need only shed water (not snow), and masonry construction (rather than the brick of the North) are as sensible in our day as they were one hundred years ago.

Miami, alternately shameless and discreet, is a city of paradoxes. Its climate fosters openness while its energy code calls for enclosure. Its natives seek a sense of history while its immigrants quest for a future. Founded on real estate fantasies, it is contending with many of today's harshest urban and social realities. Some of the solutions Miami succeeds in finding may become solutions for the problems other American cities will face in the coming decades. This challenge explains to a great degree the exuberance with which Miamians live and design their homes. Today's Miami is exciting—with an energy that is far different from the Miami of my childhood.

With perhaps as many design possibilities at hand as there are varieties of plant life, Miami may well be one of this country's most vivid examples of adaptability—to climate, to shifts in population, to evolution in style. The lessons Miami offers are crucial, as the planet changes faster year by year, growing more crowded and heating up.

White buildings stand out in memory when I think of a younger Miami. White, like tennis  togs—clean, cool, and  classic. White, like the facades of early Miami Beach hotels  and apartments,

rdensely clustered against the uninterrupted blue of sea and sky. White  worked beautifully in this small-scale  neighborhood

—just as it does in the Aegean, where villas, built nearly on top of one another, allow no green or flowering color to grow between structures and complicate the palette. The effect is sparkling and pristine.

Today, however, color is fashionable . . . and powerful. In the early 1980s, the interior designer Leonard Horowitz painted the facades of a host of Miami Beach Art Deco hotels in tones of deep pink and creamy turquoise. The impact of these novel colors on the historic buildings brought more attention to the landmark district than years of political activity had been able to generate. Though now overused, the Necco wafer hues created a critical visual mass and thereby served to help the public and the city government recognize an architectural treasure it had long overlooked.

The television show "Miami Vice" took the reinterpreted Deco look even further and amplified the style with its own distinctive palette. "Deco pink" became so popular a choice for Miami architecture that soon everything from apartment buildings and suburban ranch houses to office buildings and warehouses was awash in flamingo tones. Pink, in fact, became the beige of the eighties. At the same time, the architectural firm Arquitectonica, interested in making their buildings identifiable from the expressway, painted a series of Brickell Avenue high-rise condominiums with blues, reds, and yellows that appeared to have been selected straight off the basic color wheel. Suddenly, steamy, screaming primaries and biting color schemes were the vogue.

Miami is one of the few cities in this country

hues resonate against a cooling backdrop of green and blue.

that can comfortably host so large a spectrum —everything from pastels to deeply saturated Caribbean colors. Some find the use of dark tones a radical gesture in this bright climate. Others find soft, sweet hues inappropriate. The interior designer Dennis Jenkins, for example, believes that pastels have little place here because, in the tropics and subtropics, tones in nature are much deeper. The color of water, he points out, ranges from deep aqua to dark purple, and, he feels, it makes more sense to use the copper hues found in the Caribbean and Latin America. Jenkins incorporates these, as well as purple and brown tones, in his work because they diminish the intensity of the glaring subtropical sun and promote a greater sense of shade than pinks and violets, which exist only as accents, not as expanses, in nature.

Like its transient population and its constantly evolving horizon, this city's taste in architectural color changes rapidly. The city's youth is one reason: It was born in a century greedy for style and enamored of speed, and all the elements of its nature lend themselves to continual transformation.

In Miami the seasons shift not  by changes in foliage or in temperature, but by dramatic modulation in the color of the light. In its clear, dry winters, Miami is bathed in a light as golden as that  of the south of France; in summer the atmosphere turns white warm—are different from those in the rest of the country.

When the cast of humidity lifts and Miami's skies perform, they are as spectacular and fanciful as those of a Fragonard painting: Sunrises and sunsets soak the horizon with mango-colored clouds; daylight fills the sky with a blue as luminous as a Maxfield Parrish painting.

 with humidity. Even Miami's gray skies—cushiony and

Miamians have looked to a number of elements and devices as means of capitalizing on

Luminous clouds animate the horizon in

these special qualities. When glass block was introduced in the 1930s as an industrial product, Miami's builders were quick to recognize that its unique combination of translucency and strength made it an ideal material for local houses. Used first in the hotels, apartments, and winter homes of Miami Beach, glass block enhanced the nautical look of the resort. Later, in suburbs where contemporary houses were designed with open plans that merged living and dining rooms (and sometimes kitchen), glass block dividers became a practical means of defining spaces without enclosing them. Today glass block is chosen for its utility as well as its Art Deco charm.

With light, of course, comes heat, and Miami home owners have had to find means of admitting one without the other: deep overhanging eaves, jalousied windows, and blinds keep breezes moving and filter light.

Even Miami's nights owe something to the dazzling light of its days. Garden rooms suffused with candlelight gain a tropical glow. Art Deco lamps, Mediterranean torchères, modern sconces, and inset neon all fit comfortably in this city's casual decorating style.

daily virtuoso performances.

Almost anything grows . . . at an

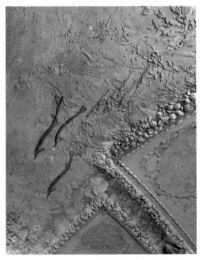

alarming rate and to an alarming size.

has so welcomed biomorphic ornamentation. Ceilings encrusted with shells are the literal interpretation of a rococo detail. Seahorses, palm trees, and fish of all varieties are depicted in carved mantelpieces, while the actual "big catch" often hangs above it. So exaggerated is the natural environment that even jungle beasts and other wild images look quite at home here.

25

TEXTURE

Because of the stripped-down, streamlined nature of most Miami interiors, walls, floors, and ceilings take on extra significance. For creative effect, designers have used unusual approaches with conventional materials, experiment- ing with tile, terrazzo, stucco, marble, and even linoleum to enliven indoor and outdoor spaces. These textures heighten Miami's sensual appeal.

Ceramic tile, a traditional Mediterranean material, was found to be perfectly suited to the subtropics. Cool, durable, and easy to maintain, it is available in a range of colors, patterns, and finishes. Simple terra-cotta tile provides elegant flooring for every style, from formal  Vizcaya-like resi- dences to Coral Gables bungalows; bold iridescent tiles decorate every surface, from kitchen counters to gar- den walls. Even linoleum finds new life in this setting.

Another stylistic element inherited from the Mediter- ranean tradition is stucco, a cement-based exterior plaster that is a low-tech solution to a high-tech dream. It was first promoted by French Mod- ernist architect Le Corbusier as part of his "industrial aesthetic." Unlike stucco exteriors in the dry Southwest and southern California, which can be treated with washes and stains or left to weather naturally, Miami's stucco facades must be painted for protection from humidity. Terrazzo, a mix- ture of cement and marble chips, has been a popular

The spectrum of surfaces ranges from jagged coral rock

to smooth terrazzo.

choice for flooring since the days of the first Art Deco hotels on Miami Beach. Terrazzo was introduced to Miami in 1926 by Louis Toffoli, founder of Miami's American Tile and Terrazzo, and it quickly won the favor of designers. It was chosen not only because it worked well in the climate, but because it offered an inexpensive means of adding beautiful decorative designs to lobby floors. Today terrazzo comes in a multitude of colors and can be laid in any pattern. After several decades of obscurity, terrazzo is experiencing a revival.

M
EDIT

ERRRANEAN

*m*uch of the distinctive character of Miami's architecture, from its early years to the present day, has derived from the picturesque Mediterranean tradition. The

Spanish, who came to Florida in the 16th century, brought with them a *style*

building style that had developed for centuries in the hot climates of the Iberian peninsula, southern

Italy, and North Africa: thick masonry walls to

keep interiors cool by day and warm by night; small windows to discourage heat, dust, and marauders; and inner courtyards for privacy, protection, and shelter from the elements. Most of these features are better suited to arid rather than humid atmospheres like Florida's and require construction materials, such as stone and adobe, that are scarce in southern Florida's swampy, sandy terrain. Although true Mediterranean architecture never became established here for these and other reasons, the Spanish colonial heritage was influential. Miami's design pioneers in the early part of this century not only incorporated breezeways, overhangs, and setback windows—practical elements for shade and ventilation—from Mediterranean models, they also created pastiches of romantic effects that evoked, rather than reproduced, the Mediterranean style by using features such as barrel-tiled roofs, Moorish towers, sculpted heraldry over windows and doors, and colorful glazed tiles and mosaics on walls and floors.

Vizcaya, James Deering's winter estate on Biscayne Bay, built in 1914, and its neighboring early-20th-century villas were likely the first Mediterranean-style structures erected in Miami. The highest concentration of this architecture, however, lies not on Biscayne Bay but in Coral Gables. The city's founder, George Merrick, gave this 20th-century development a 20th-century interpretation. A dreamer, poet, and entrepreneur, Merrick was probably America's first modern land developer. In the early 1920s he parlayed the Miami grapefruit plantation left him as part of his father's estate into a landmark planned community and Florida's first land-speculation deal. His dream, only partly realized, transformed his 1,600-acre truck farm into a brand-new city of Old World charm.

Convinced Miami would "provide a natural setting with which Mediterranean architecture would harmonize," Merrick conjured up a place as fantastic as a Busby Berkeley set, with buildings plucked from Spanish, Italian,

37

Moorish, Dutch, and Chinese sources. With his mother's native pink limestone house in mind, he called his city Coral Gables.

In a real estate saga that has few parallels, Merrick first subdivided his property into commercial, residential, and resort areas, then carved out a system of winding Venetian-style waterways—which he stocked with twenty-five gondolas and gondoliers —that led to the "South Sea islands of Coral Gables," Tahiti Beach. These canals also allowed him to advertise his city as having "more than 40 miles of waterfront." To attract wealthy residents, Merrick commissioned Schultze and Weaver, architects of New York's Pierre, Sherry-Netherland, and Waldorf-Astoria hotels, Palm Beach's The Breakers, and other renowned resorts, to design a lavish hotel for the Gables called the Biltmore. Today, refurbished and operating again as a resort hotel, the Biltmore boasts, among other dramatic features, a copper-clad 315-foot tower that replicates the Giralda bell tower of Seville.

Nearby, Merrick transformed an abandoned quarry into a spectacular swimming hole, the Venetian pool. After luring prospective buyers to Miami with glamorous advertisements that cost him more than $3 million a year, Merrick hired William Jennings Bryan—for a fee of $100,000—to stand at the gates of the Venetian Pool and, in his renowned oratorical style, sell Coral Gables lots.

To distinguish his city from the rest of Miami, Merrick asked the artist Denman Fink, the landscape architect Frank Button, and the architects Walter de Garmo and Phineas Paist to design special concrete and coral rock entrances. He also commissioned a number of monumental fountains—all crafted from locally quarried coral rock—to augment the Gables' Spanish aura.

Merrick's real estate business was ruined by the devastating 1926 hurricane and the 1929 stock market crash. Nevertheless, Coral Gables survives—a unique community of gracefully aging Mediterranean-style homes.

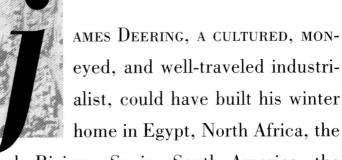

jAMES DEERING, A CULTURED, MONeyed, and well-traveled industrialist, could have built his winter home in Egypt, North Africa, the French Riviera, Spain, South America, the South Seas, or the Orient—in any warm exotic spot anywhere in the world. He chose 180 acres of isolated mangrove and hardwood hammock in one of the least civilized regions of 20th-century America—Miami.

In 1914, Deering broke ground for a seventy-

Villa on Biscayne Bay

A French-inspired teahouse, LEFT, *stands at the end of the seawall promenade of Villa Vizcaya.* ABOVE, *a view of the Italian Renaissance–style estate from the garden.*

room Italian Renaissance–style villa that would become one of this country's great houses. Most of the mansions erected between the Civil War and the Great Depression were sprawling and extravagant—the "cottages" of Newport, the voluptuous salons of Fifth Avenue, and such monuments to grandeur and excess as San Simeon. Vizcaya, as Deering called his winter home, using the Basque word for "elevated place," stands as a rare example of restrained good taste, appreciation of history, and sensitivity to nature. Today a museum open to the public and rentable for large parties, Vizcaya is testimony to Deering's own sensibilities and to the talents of the men he chose to design it. First was Paul Chalfin, a painter, designer, and curator who was introduced to Deering by the noted interior designer of the era, Elsie de Wolfe. Next, Deering commissioned the architect F. Burral Hoffman, Jr., a Harvard graduate who, like Chalfin, had studied at the Ecole des Beaux-Arts in Paris, to design the house. For the gardens, he hired Diego Suarez, a Colombian-born, Italian-trained landscape architect.

Centered on a large atrium (recently covered with glass in order to control the effects of humidity on the house's prized furniture and art), each of Vizcaya's four sides is an independent architectural composition focusing on a different period of the Renaissance. The entrance loggia, dominated by a marble statue of Bacchus standing above a carved marble 2nd-century Roman tub, leads to the entrance hall, decorated in the style of the French Empire. From here, the rooms follow *enfilade*, from one theme and time to another.

The formal Neoclassical library, for example, is decorated in 18th-century Robert Adam

Travels throughout Europe observing domestic architecture enabled designer Paul Chalfin to give each of Vizcaya's rooms authentic period detailing. Most of the house's wall panels, ceilings, mantels, wrought-iron grilles, furniture, rugs, tapestries, and artwork were purchased abroad.

style; the reception room reflects the frivolous life of mid-17th-century aristocracy. In the mid-18th-century Italian Rococo music room, the paneled walls and ceilings are decorated with shells, coral, and curious marine life appropriate to an Italian villa by the sea. The formal banquet hall is furnished with elaborately carved 15th- and 16th-century pieces. The light-filled tea room is decorated with 18th-century Neapolitan murals, a richly colored marble floor, a Nubian marble mantelpiece, and ornamental stained-glass doors.

The original garden design of Villa Vizcaya centered on a 10-acre formal garden, which incorporated a French parterre, an arrangement of low, clipped curvilinear hedges; a fountain garden designed like an ancient Persian garden; a theater garden for music and entertainment; a secret garden with walls of locally quarried limestone; a maze; a lagoon; tropical outer gardens connected by bridges; a boathouse with a roof garden; and winding drives through groves of palm and other varieties of trees.

To synthesize these diverse and luxurious elements, Diego Suarez devised a fan-shaped plan that continued the north-south axis of the house, symmetrically balancing its architectural features and incorporating expansive vistas within a complex design of intermingling parterres and long-reaching allées. The effect is symphonic, a harmony of Italian Renaissance design, baroque curves, and French intricacy. Yet the clarity of the landscape design, as with the architecture of the house, precludes the disorder that could so easily result from mixing so many styles. Suarez's brilliance lay not only in the scope and detailing of his plan, but in his adaptation of Italian hill design to accommodate tropical vegetation. Instead of traditional boxwood hedges, he planted fragrant jasmine; for his high hedges, he used the prevalent Australian pine.

In addition to these superb natural and ar-

The marble walls of
Deering's own bath, LEFT,
are decorated with
Sheffield silver plaques
and a custom-designed
shaving stand with running
water, in front of doors to
a balcony overlooking
Biscayne Bay.
ABOVE, one of the carved
limestone entrances leads
to the grottoes.

45

chitectural elements, the gardens are further distinguished by hundreds of ornaments procured or commissioned by Paul Chalfin. In the tradition of Versailles, he graced the walk and gardens with life-size statues of mythological figures—Jupiter, Mars, Venus, and Adonis. To add height, he set out columns—sixteen of indigenous limestone, fourteen imported from Europe, and two excavated from ancient Roman ruins.

It took nearly eight years to complete Vizcaya's grounds, and required eighty people to maintain the finished garden and working farm to James Deering's standards. New flowers opened daily, to Deering's delight (flowers for cutting were raised in the greenhouses, never taken from the formal gardens), and water lilies floated in his reflecting pool. Sadly, Deering was to savor the pleasures of his private Eden for only two years. He died of a ruptured appendix while returning from Europe on the S.S. *Paris* in 1925. Then, in 1926, a hurricane ravaged Vizcaya's grounds. Nothing of the original scale was ever attempted here again.

Frogs and lizards by Charles Cary Rumsey embellish a sarcophagus-shaped fountain basin, ABOVE. *The Secret Garden, inspired by that of Villa Gamberaia, near Florence, Italy,* RIGHT, *leads to the bay. It is approached through the arches,* BELOW, *which are framed in rusticated limestone.*

Caribbean-yellow walls, framed in white, surround an antique wicker love seat in the Florida room, OPPOSITE. *Mediterranean details include stucco walls, barrel tiles, and arches,* INSETS OPPOSITE, TOP, AND ABOVE.

Room to Breathe

t HE SMALL ROOMS AND SMALL WINdows common to Miami's early Spanish-style bungalows often make these houses dark and dowdy. The modest 1926 Coral Gables house now owned by the architects Thomas Coppage and Oswald Leal was just such an example. To let in the light, Coppage and Leal added French doors and single-hung windows; to enhance the existing light, they relied on color: white in the living room—where repainted, refinished plaster walls and bleached hardwood floors lend a feeling of clean modernity—and sharp yellow on the porch, where the intensity of the color is as refreshing as it is surprising. Here they also restored the arches, which had been "plugged" by a previous owner, and laid a white-speckled tile floor.

The owners kept furnishings simple. On the porch, antique wicker chairs are old-fashioned and romantic. Inside, a small glass-block and sheet-glass cocktail table and chairs, love seats, and cushions covered in cotton reinforce the interior's crispness.

Because the house is set on a tiny lot, they

had to take ingenious measures to increase privacy, planting their garden intensively, eschewing grass for a ground cover of cypress

mulch. Boston and asparagus ferns grow close to the house, and grander areca palms, Alexander palms, and Chinese palms flourish around the perimeter.

The owners stripped and bleached the floors through-out the house. The plain lines of tables and chairs, ABOVE, ABOVE LEFT, AND LEFT, *accentuate the architectural simplicity of the rooms. The Zenith clock,* OPPOSITE, *dates from the 1950s and was a gift from a client.*

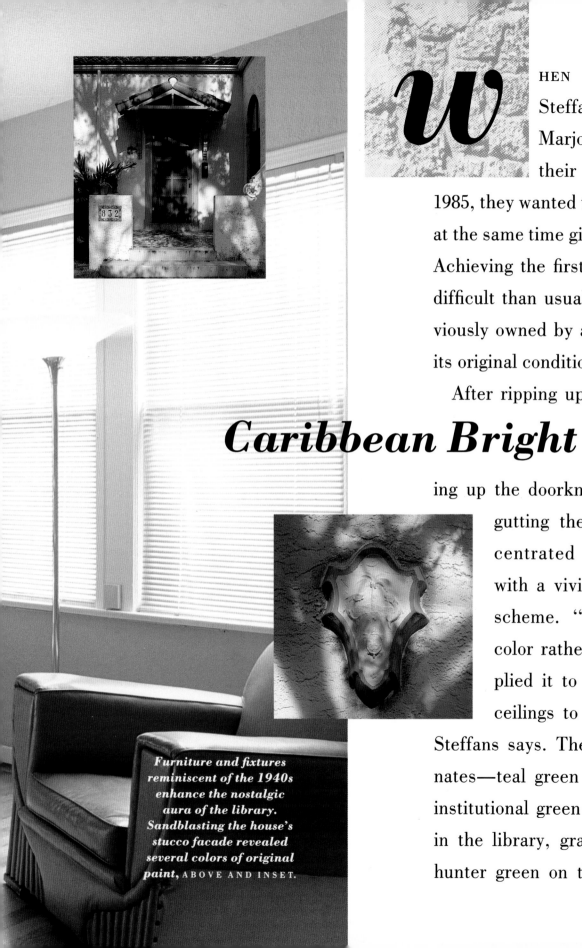

*Furniture and fixtures
reminiscent of the 1940s
enhance the nostalgic
aura of the library.
Sandblasting the house's
stucco facade revealed
several colors of original
paint,* ABOVE AND INSET.

Caribbean Bright

*W*HEN THE ARCHITECT MICHAEL Steffans and the interior designer Marjorie Goldman moved into their 1926 Coral Gables house in 1985, they wanted to "restore it accurately, yet at the same time give it a feeling of the 1980s." Achieving the first goal turned out to be less difficult than usual, since the house was previously owned by a blind family who left it in its original condition.

After ripping up the carpeting, which concealed handsome Dade County pine floors, cleaning up the doorknobs and drawer pulls, and gutting the kitchen, the couple concentrated on updating the house with a vivid, Caribbean-derived color scheme. "We chose bright, intense color rather than soft pastels and applied it to everything from walls and ceilings to window trims and doors," Steffans says. The green spectrum predominates—teal green on the bedroom walls, an institutional green in the kitchen, lime green in the library, gray green in the office, and hunter green on the doors—with accents of

53

Wedgwood blue on the porch ceiling and ocher on window and door trims. The concentration of many deep, rich colors in a modest space creates a range of moods that change from soothing to stimulating according to the intensity of the light.

The décor also reflects Steffans's and Goldman's interest in balancing new and old. Thus, upholstered armchairs and rattan furniture, influenced by design trends of the 1940s, are juxtaposed against stainless-steel kitchen appliances, modern bathroom fixtures, and sleek Italian lamps.

French doors open the unairconditioned dining room to cooling breezes, ABOVE. *The owners gave the classic checkerboard pattern a modern twist,* OPPOSITE, *by painting the squares Mediterranean yellow and green. Pots and pans hang in the kitchen,* INSET AND TOP.

A coffee table is a marble top on recycled columns, FAR LEFT. *The Tuscan red fireplace,* LEFT, *had been painted baby blue by previous owners. After sandblasting the front porch,* RIGHT, *Steffans and Goldman left the raw stucco exposed, revealing several colors of original paint. In the bedroom,* BELOW, *they applied a cooling teal green.*

i F, BY SOME TWIST OF TIME AND CIR-cumstance, Catalan architect Antonio Gaudí could have designed a subtropical residence for Federico Fellini, the result might be a setting as vivid, absorbing, and filled with visual extravagance as Villa Malaga, the home of the interior designer Dennis Jenkins and the decorative-tile showroom owner Sunny McLean. The present guise of this once small and boxy Spanish-style house, built in 1926, illustrates Jenkins's conviction

An Environment of Art

A stucco wall embedded with tile shards, OPPOSITE, *fanciful plywood palm trees designed by Richard Bugdal,* ABOVE, *and hand-painted tiles, such as the bee,* ABOVE RIGHT, *characterize the colorful exaggeration of the garden. Tapered, Babylonian-style columns,* RIGHT, *herald the entrance to Villa Malaga.*

that the home is the best possible outlet for personal expression. In fact, he has fashioned his residence with such exuberance—lavishing upon it twelve years of coloring, carving, shaping, and shifting—that he considers it "an environmental art form." As a result, nearly every corner has both historical allusions and richly textured, colorful surfaces.

Jenkins and McLean arranged the original

four-bedroom, two-bath plan into a villagelike collage of rooms and passages. From the front of the house through the interior and out to the courtyard, the rooms lead through a sequence of cultural references into a garden that exuberantly celebrates Miami's florid subtropical botany and outdoor lifestyle.

The street exterior, with its stone driveway and stucco walls, is what Jenkins calls a "tip of the hat to Rome." Inside, textured, tinted walls, plastered to resemble limestone, simulate those of the houses of Pompeii. Geometric patterns have been stenciled across some walls and thick layers of plaster shaped across others. The surfaces look rough but feel soft— a contradiction that appeals to Jenkins. "You can't stand at arm's length from interiors," he says. "We need relationships with our living spaces that are tactile as well as visual."

To conceal the main air-conditioning unit, Jenkins designed a fir-slatted ceiling that visually alludes to the thatched-roof log houses of nomadic Indians. "What I really want are logs and twigs," he expains, "but since we're no longer wanderers, this is my way of symbolizing that aspect of our history."

Broken tile enlivens exterior walls, ABOVE. *African art combines with Mexican cantera floors,* OPPOSITE, *in an interior that emphasizes nature and tactility.*

The garden ensemble comprises French leather-wrapped wicker chairs and a hand-painted table. RIGHT, *a detail of a wall mural and a wooden cabinet painted by Richard Warholic for Antares.*

The living room, kitchen, and rear bedroom open onto a landscaped courtyard connected by an explosion of color. The bedroom—originally the garage—remains an independent structure. Although the absence of a covered passageway exposes the owners to the elements whenever they move between rooms, they prefer the physical detachment. "Even though it's only a matter of fourteen feet, we're literally apart from the cares and concerns of the household," says McLean.

Here, in the courtyard and bedroom, vibrant bougainvillea, caladiums, and impatiens extend the palette from the golds of antiquity to the bright, glare-diminishing hues of the Caribbean. Inside, wall murals of red, yellow, and blue depict benevolent voodoo gods.

Most of the decorative applications used in Villa Malaga, such as stenciling and texturing, required little expense. Some even demanded little expertise. Yet all are effective in lending character. As Jenkins says, "Everywhere you turn, a surface is saying something."

The checkerboard, Jenkins's signature motif, fills the bath, ABOVE, *and the bedroom, originally a detached garage,* RIGHT. *The "wall of life" painted by artist Ellen Moss, depicts Haitian religious scenes. Over the bed is the Haitian voodoo god of the universe. Rattan stools from Sunny McLean and Co. stand before the vanity,* BELOW.

*m*ost of Miami's wood-frame bungalows can be found in Coconut

Grove, a wooded enclave

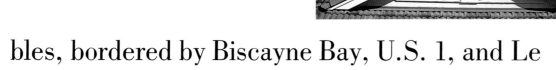

located between down-

town Miami and Coral Ga-

bles, bordered by Biscayne Bay, U.S. 1, and Le

G A L O W

Jeune Road. One of the earliest settlements in

southern Florida, the Grove *style*

was established long before there existed a City

of Miami. It was first settled in the mid-1800s

...en, lighthouse keepers, and seamen ...o the area to salvage the millions of ...rth of vessels that shipwrecked on ...lorida reef. Eventually, it grew to ...e of the region's most spirited, in- ...nd diversified communities.

...e notable Coconut Grove pioneers ...odore Ralph Middleton Munroe of ...d, New York, a ...seaworthy, shal- ...ats. Munroe en- ...ting the shoals, ...reefs along the ...., and after win- ...remote outpost ...rs, moved here ...Undaunted by ...es, hurricanes, and isolation, he ...y house on Biscayne Bay (now ...Barnacle and open to the public ...to which he applied his experi- ...builder and his knowledge and ...f the surroundings. To protect ...m hurricanes, he set its pine ...reated with crude oil to resist termites—deep into the ground. Bolted to this

foundation were the structure's supports, made of lumber salvaged from wrecked ships.

So enthusiastic was Munroe about the natural beauty of Coconut Grove that he convinced fellow settlers Charles and Isabella Peacock to build a hotel here in 1882. The Peacock Inn, the first hotel on the southern Florida mainland, became the core of what, by the turn of the century, had grown into a thriving community populated by black Bahamians, Key West natives (known as "Conchs"), and New England intellectuals. Eventually, the Grove's reputation as an individualist's paradise in a sultry climate attracted the attention of giants of industry and letters. Men of wealth and influence, such as James Deering, William Matheson, and David Fairchild, developed magnificent properties that replaced the pioneer houses and wild mangroves. Today, their estates—Vizcaya, Matheson Hammock, and Fairchild Tropical Garden —are among Miami's, and the country's, most admired public parks.

Throughout the first several decades of the 1900s, frame vernacular houses came to be common throughout Coconut Grove. The one- and two-story wood frame dwellings reflected the simple quality of life here: they used available building materials, usually Dade County pine in which the resin was allowed to harden, making the wood impervious to termites and fire, and were ornamented with jigsaw traceries under eaves and on porch railings. Steeply pitched roofs drew warm air upward, one-story front porches allowed relief from indoor temperatures, and the pattern of windows and doors encouraged cross-ventilation. When the house had several rooms or more, mounting on piers prevented dry rot; the larger houses stood on masonry piers, the smaller on lime rock or cypress.

Bungalows, the first popular residential style of this country's rising middle class, also proved ideal for the Miami climate. These street-facing vernacular residences were customarily planned with a sprawling horizontal ground floor, a recessed upper story that provided a sleeping porch, and an overhanging roof that sheltered a veranda and often continued to form a porte-cochere. These simple, broad-gabled houses, with their unpainted floors and walls, had deep porches with wide eaves that blocked high-angle summer sun. Numerous windows admitted low-angle winter sunlight for warmth while providing summertime cross-ventilation.

One of the most notable and well-preserved examples of bungalow housing in Miami is, surprisingly, the childhood home of George Merrick, pioneer of Mediterranean-style Coral Gables. Built in 1899 by Merrick's father, this gabled, wood-frame two-story Massachusetts colonial–style bungalow had high ceilings and double-hung windows. In recent years, it has been restored to its earlier grace and opened to the public.

Today these early bungalows are practical, comfortable, and adaptable, lending themselves to a variety of interpretations.

Tropical Tree House

The ultimate getaway, this colorful stilt house nestled in a grove of sabal palms, A B O V E, *looks like a Technicolor version of* The Swiss Family Robinson. *The sleeping porch,* O P P O S I T E, *is used year round. Dolphin and heron motifs,* R I G H T, *were carved from untrimmed floor beams.*

eILEEN AND PAUL ARSENAULT'S PRImary concern for their weekend home south of Miami in the Keys was that their "touch" on the unspoiled site "be as light as possible." It was the solitude and virgin spirit of the land that attracted them, qualities they were determined not only to preserve but to honor. The result is a tree house, set on stilts in a grove of sabal palms, and with features that intrude as little as possible into the environment: a cistern collects rainwater for cooking and bathing; solar panels provide enough electricity to run ceiling fans and reading lights.

The Arsenaults' original plan was to build a simple, high-ceilinged painting studio for Paul that included a porch with a built-in bed and a kitchen with a wraparound porch. They took their idea to the artist Dale Beatty, whose unusual 12 × 20-foot "Jamaican cook shack" nearby they admired. Beatty

In the kitchen, LEFT AND ABOVE, *the pre-electric refrigerator and 1930s stove run on propane. An heirloom quilt covers the studio couch,* OPPOSITE, *and a kilim and 1940s fabric are used on the living room seating,* OPPOSITE ABOVE.

conceived a simple design—two connected pods set at angles to each other—and built the house himself. The process, he claims, "defied educated carpentry. It was a case where artistic carpentry ruled."

This approach particularly dominates in the carved floor beams shaped with a jigsaw into dolphin and heron motifs. "People forget that the base of a building, particularly of a stilt house, can be embellished as easily as the top," says Beatty. He used raw yellow pine throughout, pressure-treated on the exterior, untreated inside. Paul and Eileen chose bright Caribbean colors for outside walls and trim and used the same colors as accents on the interior. Inside wood surfaces were either painted or pickled (an application in which pigment is mixed with mineral spirits and then applied with a rag) for a soft look.

Sleeping porches and shutters enable the house to be used year round. Breezes and ceiling fans cool the rooms in summer, and decoratively painted shutters shut out cold winds in winter.

The artist Dale Beatty carved the wooden base of the table that furnishes the wraparound porch off the kitchen, LEFT. *Views of the surrounding island jungle from every room add to the house's airy feel,* ABOVE. *Throughout, the interior wood has been pickled in the Caribbean colors that Arsenault encountered during travels in the islands.*

ONCE A WICKED-LOOKING WRECK with a collapsed foundation, rotted roof, treacherous floors, and fifteen tons of trash inside, this hundred-year-old house could have been salvaged only by the visionaries Craig Biondi and Gregory Forsyth. Nevertheless, the two frequently thought their vision was folly: "People would grimace when they asked us how long until we'd move in . . . and we'd already been living in the house for six months," describes Biondi. Yet 5½ years of labor and sawdust proved them geniuses of reclamation.

Centenarian Reclamation

Greg Forsyth used palm fronds as stencils and spray-painted the table and chairs, OPPOSITE. *The owners built the timber deck,* RIGHT, *themselves. It wraps around the pool, barely visible behind the surrounding foliage.*

Searching for an inexpensive house with a yard big enough for a pool, Biondi and Forsyth purchased the two-story, four-bedroom structure in 1982. Lacking any prior building experience, they had planned to hire professionals to do the restoration work, but quickly changed their minds when they received the high-priced estimates. Realizing they had undertaken a marathon en-

The honey-colored wood walls, once obscured by twenty-five layers of paint, ABOVE, are the homeowners' greatest pride. A hand-painted multicolored finish updates an old glass-fronted chest, RIGHT. The colors of the glazed Chinese ceramic ware in the living room, OPPOSITE, complement both the tone of the walls and vivid hues in Biondi's oversize mango paintings.

deavor, they decided to install the pool as soon as the house reached livable standards, an approach they highly recommend to other Florida renovators. "Even though the place was a mess, we could jump into the water whenever we felt exhausted from fixing," says Forsyth. "Floating around on a raft, the project wouldn't seem so overwhelming."

After they had cleared away the trash, they faced the removal of twenty-five layers of paint from the Dade County pine walls. Although it required months of sandblasting, Forsyth loved the process, as well as the result, because "it made it smell so good."

Replacing the floor with pressure-treated 1 × 6 pine planks, Biondi and Forsyth then stained them with a translucent glaze of enamel and polyurethane. They used a white finish downstairs and burgundy upstairs in the master bedroom, a room they made spacious by combining two smaller bedrooms.

Construction experts laid foundations and put up the roof, but the homeowners added new siding and windows, as well as new beams to support the badly bowed ceiling, without outside help. Under an extension of the roof at

the rear of the house they constructed a spacious deck around the pool.

To give the house the Victorian look appropriate to its vintage, they used ornate wood railings left over from the building of a nearby new resort along the front and rear porches, on the interior stairs, and in the yard as fencing. Forsyth salvaged the gingerbread that embellishes windows from the trash of another old house in renovation.

Once the structural work was completed, Biondi and Forsyth concentrated on the interior, transforming the house into a colorful gallery of Biondi's striking canvases. They also employed their talents to marbleize furniture, columns, and even the master bedroom's walls. Biondi designed the bedroom quilts.

Besides the pool, the owners' favorite part of the house is the dining porch. "Putting the dining table out here was one of the smartest things we did," says Biondi. "Alluring as all the rooms are, there's nothing like sharing a meal al fresco, surrounded by your own garden. And with this wonderful climate, we can use the porch for dining all but maybe ten nights of the year."

The furnishings of the upstairs front porch—two butterfly chairs and a hammock—make clear that this open-air room, OPPOSITE, *is designed strictly for relaxation. Craig Biondi's oil paintings of tropical plants and fruit,* ABOVE, *mirror the house's real-life decoration.*

mOVING TO THE SUBTROPICS GAVE Chicago interior designer and entrepreneur Stefano Marchetti a perfect excuse to decorate a year-round home as a beach house. A fanciful environment of improvised charm, the house is full of surprises. Here

an eclectic variety of furnishings culled from flea markets coexists with pieces from Marchetti's "closet of mistakes" (furniture once intended for clients' houses).

The Personal Beach

From tableaux to landscape, the Marchetti bungalow, ABOVE RIGHT, *pays homage to nature. The sago palms arranged in a still life,* LEFT, *can be preserved for months. Palms, Spanish bayonet, and bougainvillea grow vigorously in the sandy garden,* INSETS BELOW.

Marchetti worked with his brother Paul to restore and furnish the "structurally sound but cosmetically shabby" 1927 Conch house. "Never did we sit down and draw up rooms as we do for clients," he says with a laugh. "Here it was whatever we could get our hands on." That meant everything from a Caribbean faux bamboo armoire to an obelisk bought in Key West to 1950s Sicilian terra-cotta pots. Colorful tropical paintings by local artist Craig Biondi hang both inside and out.

The most notable feature of the property is

a manmade "beach," Marchetti's solution to a massive gully filled with trash and overgrown with insidious Brazilian pepper trees, which ran through the property. Even after endless hauling and hacking, the ravine still looked like a dump, Marchetti says. Rather than fight it, he decided to bury it. He filled the gully with load after load of rocky soil in a process that took five years: "The fill takes time to settle, and if you try to add it all at once, it forms sink holes." Eventually, he topped the fill with crushed coral and a periodically renewed layer of sand for whiteness. The finished landscape suggests a short walk to a nonexistent body of water, and enhances the sense of surprise that is the house's most important asset.

Marchetti created his own soil through years of mulching, and added Alexander palms, traveler's palms, and giant birds-of-paradise.

Found objects, including a carved-wood boar from Florence, are arranged on a table on the porch, FAR LEFT. *The vertical rhythms of a traveler's palm repeat the lines in the wood banister,* ABOVE. *Fencing,* LEFT, *is made of pressure-treated pine.*

I N A WORLD KNOWN FOR ITS HUES OF mint, shocking pink, turquoise, and of course dazzling white, the house of the Miami architect Mark Hampton comes as a dramatic revelation. Hidden in a garden so thick with tropical and subtropical foliage that it can almost be called a jungle, Hampton's house is painted black so that it virtually disappears in its surroundings. When he bought the property in the early 1970s, he was at first attracted not so much to the house as to the potential for creating a dense garden on the grounds where the original oaks and palms offered an ideal backdrop. The house, nevertheless, appealed to Hampton's modern sensibilities—it was painted black on the outside and white on the inside—a house turned inside out.

House in a Hammock

Orchids, begonias, crotons, and rare palms fill the cultivated hammock surrounding the house of the Miami architect Mark Hampton.

In planning the interior, the architect kept the feeling of the bungalow modest with elegant classic modern furniture. The effect of this understatement is to focus attention on the splendors of the garden. Every room overlooks a tangle of bromeliads, or-

*In contrast to the black
exterior, the interior walls
of the bungalow are
painted a clean, restful
white,* LEFT AND
OPPOSITE. *Because he
prefers a clear view of the
garden, Hampton removed
the screens from all
windows and doors. Two
Le Corbusier chairs in
the living room,*
ABOVE, *define the home's
quiet modernity.*

chids, and large-leafed native plants beneath a canopy of live oaks. To capitalize on these views, Hampton removed the screens from his windows: "In the heat I keep the house air-conditioned and the windows closed; in the cool months, there are no bugs."

From the beginning, Hampton's plan for the garden was to cultivate it along the lines of a natural hammock—a dense wood with thick tree cover and understory foliage. He planted low-growing trees, such as tree ferns, orange jasmine (generally used elsewhere as a bush), ligustrum, stoppers, and crotons—trees that never grow higher than 20 feet—and smaller plants, such as bromeliads, *Rhapis* palms, cycads, *Monstera deliciosa*, heliconia, and ground-growing ficus vines. Next, he laid a maze of paths of light-colored pearock edged with local oolitic rock that darkens with age.

Hampton points out that the subtle effect of gray green Bismarckia and light green *Licuala grandis* and *Licuala spinosa* against darker green palms. The only accent colors are derived from the mottled magentas and oranges of the crotons, the vivid reds and oranges of heliconia blossoms, and the orange jasmine

flowers. Blue ginger, a ground cover that requires little sun, is the only brilliant color. Form and texture provide the garden's emphatic contrasts: solitaire palms with loose, hanging leaves against slender, erect Chinese fan palms, and the oversize foliage of Bismarckia against tiny leaves of live oak.

Throughout this landscape, majestic, straight-trunked royal palms zoom toward the sky. Against the black backdrop of the house, the greens become ever more vibrant.

The black exterior of the house is a radical departure from the typical subtropical white and Caribbean pastels. Hampton likes the way the dark tone merges with the shadowy garden.

Downtown Beach House

Gingerbread and a tropically unruly garden lend an old-fashioned flavor to the screened wooden porch, OPPOSITE AND RIGHT. *The contoured rattan sofa,* ABOVE, *is upholstered in cotton duck.*

F ASHION MODEL TOBY WOLTERS'S octogenarian Coconut Grove cottage represents a radical departure from the formal elegance of his previous home, an antique-filled apartment in New York City. Casual as a beach house, this light, comfortable wood-frame bungalow dates at least to 1910, the year it was moved to its present ficus-shaded site.

The years have left various marks on the house, an aspect of its character Wolters enjoys. In the kitchen/dining room, for example, an earlier owner installed authentic Art Deco light sconces. In the downstairs bathroom, which was likely added in the 1930s or 1940s, a deep copper tub is set in a surround of teak that matches the wall paneling. Decorative pressed tin was used not only on ceilings, but also on walls.

Wolters didn't hesitate to add modifications of his own. He transformed an unused dormer beneath a pitched roof between two bedrooms on the second floor into a compact but unique bathroom. Outside, he turned a screened work-shop with concrete flooring into a study/guest room by enclosing the space and extending the corrugated plastic roof.

But the addition that has had "the most im-pact on the life of the house and living in it" is the deck, Wolters explains. "It's as if I've added a big outdoor living room."

To continue the casual theme, Wolters deco-rated with warm Santa Fe colors and country-as well as beach-style furnishings: a simple carpenter-made dining table in the kitchen, a canvas-covered rattan sofa and wicker chairs in the living room, and Adiron-dack chairs on the front porch. Nine ceiling fans en-able Wolters to live comfort-ably without air-conditioning.

The bathroom, ABOVE, was added in the 1930s or '40s. The mirror, LEFT, is probably a Mennonite piece from Pennsylvania. The spacious kitchen opens on to a recently added deck, RIGHT.

DECO &

the buildings were embellished with Art Deco friezes, fixtures, and ornaments of tropical interpretation. Set squarely on the flat terrain of the beach, facing the ocean breezes, the Art Deco district evokes the romance of the ocean liner with railings and porthole windows.

European Art Deco, an elegant style of furniture, fashion, graphic, and interior design that culminated in Paris during the 1920s, expressed a generation's fascination with futurism, fantasy, speed, and exoticism through a synthesis of streamlined images, exquisitely applied ornament, and rich, sensuous surfaces. In America the style romanticized this country's love affair with industry and commerce. On Miami Beach, its purpose and application were quite different.

Since their clients could not afford the precious stones and rarefied woods of European Art Deco, Miami Beach's architects turned to neon, aluminum tubing, glass block, Bakelite, Vitrolite, and paint to create a sophisticated effect. They designed porthole windows, deck-like balconies, and flagstaff finials; and had motifs such as stylized fountains, geometric wave patterns, seabirds, and tropical vegetation incised into the masonry to mirror what was, especially then, a highly exotic geography. Originally painted white with seafoam green, powder blue, and salmon pink trim, the buildings looked modern, snappy, and clean.

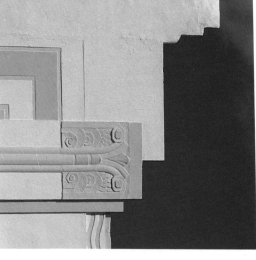

Inside, tinted terrazzo floors, Vitrolite tile walls, and sleek, stainless-steel fixtures further enhanced the Beach's cool, up-to-the-minute yet timeless sense of style.

By the time World War II halted the first construction boom on Miami Beach, the fashionability of the opulent-seeming Art Deco style had ended, and modern architecture had been imported to the United States by Walter Gropius, Mies van der Rohe, and other instructors and admirers of the German Bauhaus. True modern architecture, as these doctrinaire intellectuals practiced it, respects the tenets of Modernism espoused in the 1920s by the French architect Le Corbusier, incor-

porating horizontal bands of windows, a continuous flow of space, a flat roof (which could be used as a solarium), piers that raise the structure above ground level, and columns, rather than load-bearing walls, that support the roof without obstructing the view.

Though a bastardized version of modern architecture known as the International Style eventually became the signature style of corporate skyscrapers, German Bauhaus influence on residential design was far less profound. Nevertheless, Miami, once defined by the Deco look at the Beach and stucco and frame bungalows elsewhere, became, by the 1950s, an ever-expanding residential landscape of flat, split-level, and ranch-style houses. This is the look of Miami's suburbs today.

In the late 1940s, for the first time since the hurricane of 1926, the stock market crash of 1929, and the construction halt caused by World War II, the real estate market soared. As lumber and steel became available again

and the Veterans Administration bestowed home loans on the returning GIs who had enjoyed their stints in the sunshine, Miami's house-building flood became unstoppable. Tract communities of builder-designed, rather than architect-designed, houses began going up by the thousands.

In most cases, little thought was given to architectural aesthetics. Instead, fast, inexpensive construction and formula floor plans became the rule. Where once verandas and front porches overlooked the street, now screened-in patios were routinely affixed to the backs of houses for privacy, barbecues, and swimming pools.

A residential development of the 1950s original to southern Florida was the "Florida room," an appendage to the house enclosed on three sides with jalousie windows and connected to the house on the fourth side by a sliding glass door, usually giving on to the dining room. This informal room, the coolest in the house, was where families gathered to

watch television and socialize. With the advent of air-conditioning, the Florida room became simply a family room.

Of the handful of Miami architects of the 1940s and 1950s who planned environmentally sensitive tract houses, the most notable was Alfred Browning Parker, who designed project homes for builders such as Marston O'Neal.

In his early, speculative houses, Parker used local materials whenever possible and consistently designed economical features such as low-roof framing; centralized plumbing risers; standard cuts of lumber, hardware, and fixtures; and single large windows and doors. The ultimate cost efficiency of picture windows is debatable (they are great for views but bad for energy conservation; Miami's current building code requires smaller windows), but Parker's basic design principles are as valid today as they were forty years ago. His set of design rules made sense both architecturally and economically. They were:

▶ Keep out the sun with roof overhangs and reflect the sun's rays away from the house with white roofs and light-colored walls.

▶ Capture as much shade as possible from carports and trees.

▶ Use ample windows for cross-ventilation, the larger windows on the windward side to admit a gentle breeze and opposite smaller ones to move it out briskly.

▶ Give bedrooms two or three exposures.

▶ Use awning-type windows to provide shade and keep out summer rains.

▶ Design the house one room wide, when possible, for cross-ventilation.

▶ Site the house on its lot so that bedrooms catch the constant southeast trade winds.

▶ Keep the house as freestanding as possible so as not to block the breeze.

▶ Use masonry construction, terrazzo slabs, and closets ventilated by louvers to help prevent mildew and wood decay.

Contemporary adaptations of the traditional courtyard house have also proved successful in Miami. Not only does this scheme, which promotes ventilation, make good sense in Miami's climate, but its roots in Latin architecture make it culturally comfortable for this international city.

S OME HOMEOWNERS MOVE BECAUSE their families outgrow the living space; others, because their tastes change. For Dennis Wilhelm and Michael Kinerk, the impetus to find a new house was the size of their collection of early 20th-century decorative arts; it had overtaken nearly every spare inch of their home.

Wilhelm, Associate Registrar of the Wolfsonian Collection, and Kinerk, Director of Technology at *The Miami Herald,* looked at more than seventy houses before coming upon this spacious Mediterranean residence on Miami Beach. So captivated were they by its generous proportions and its quirky character— which derives from a combination of Spanish and Art Deco motifs—that they purchased the house within hours of seeing it.

The walls of many early Miami Beach homes were made of plaster mixed with beach sand, a lethal combination that eventually corroded

Art Deco Showplace

A Frankart fish bookend, OPPOSITE, *sets an Art Deco tone. A relief panel on the front of the house,* RIGHT, *was painted in colors chosen by designer Leonard Horowitz.* ABOVE, *the tabletop display includes a round Spartan Bluebird radio, circa 1937.*

Pieces from the owners' massive collection of Fiestaware are set out on a dining room table designed by Eldon F. Baldauf.

The owners' collection includes framed covers of 1930s issues of Fortune, ABOVE. *Coffee tables from the French Line's SS Normandy accent the cathedral-ceilinged living room,* BELOW. *A nautical Art Deco fire screen complements the original 1933 mantelpiece carving,* RIGHT.

116

much of the plumbing and wiring. This house, with its cathedral ceilings and oak floors, was in excellent condition. It also possesses a number of unique features that were of particular delight to Wilhelm and Kinerk: a moderne-looking fireplace with carved nautical frieze, a sunken bathtub on a Vitrolite dais, and pulverized keystone columns with dolphin capitals.

Most sophisticated of all the architectural devices is the semiprivate but intimate "his and hers" bedroom suite on the second floor. The suite, like something out of a *Thin Man* movie, was a trademark of C. K. Bayliss, who designed the house in 1933. These expansive quarters enabled Wilhelm to take his Art Deco bedroom set with the 14-foot-long headboard out of storage for the first time in ten years.

On the ground floor, in the adjoining living room and Florida room, a burled Carpathian elm dining table, sideboard, and serving cart by Eldon F. Baldauf are set to display the owners' collections of Fiestaware and other table accessories made during the 1920s, 1930s, and 1940s. There is even room for two pianos, one a baby grand.

The black and green Vitrolite mirror, ABOVE LEFT, *and lavender bath tiles,* LEFT, *were part of the house's original appointments. Period lacquer furniture enhances the Deco look of the bedroom suites,* ABOVE RIGHT AND BELOW.

*The jalousied dining
porch of the Martinson-
Brooke house is set in a
palm garden. Unmatched
loom chairs contribute
to the room's casual,
airy atmosphere.*

tHE CHALLENGE MET BY THE ARCHI-
tect Suzanne Martinson and the
architectural photographer Steven Brooke in remodeling their
own home was to convert a small, nondescript
1950s tract house into an open, airy residence
that accommodates three studios and
expresses the precise tastes and
broad interests of its two strong-
minded owners. Over several years,
the couple turned two of the house's

Tropical Realism

three bedrooms into work
spaces—one that serves as
Brooke's office and the other as his art studio
—and converted a small garage into Martin-

son's design studio
and office. Both
Brooke and Mar-
tinson are rigorous
about containing
their work in these
rooms, which al-
lows them to keep
the rest of their
house private.

Their screened, jalousied porch serves as a

dining room. The dining table was designed by Martinson, its wrought-iron base inspired by work of the Vienna Secessionist architect and designer Josef Hoffmann. Martinson admits to a fondness for iron and metal pieces. "Even though they may rust in Miami's wet climate and must be sanded and repainted periodically, I'm attracted to their industrial quality and relationship to the Modernist aesthetic."

Because Brooke spends so much of his time photographing professionally designed and polished interiors, he prefers a more personal and eclectic approach in his own home. The living room, which receives morning light through amply sized jalousie windows and westerly light through clerestory windows, is furnished, like the rest of the house, with one-of-a-kind pieces and classic modern chairs, many of which they had restored. The re-covered sofa was bought for its simplicity and comfort; chairs by Mies van der Rohe, Harry Bertoia, Charles Eames, Michael Thonet, and Hans Wegner, for their sculptural quality.

Martinson and Brooke also collect paintings and drawings, many of them executed by their artist friends. They are long-time collectors of

A gauzy canopy of mosquito netting, OPPOSITE, *lends a touch of romance to the garden deck. Paintings by Jean Welch on the dining porch,* ABOVE, *and in the bedroom,* BELOW, *add tropical color. A room off the kitchen,* RIGHT, *is occupied by a baby grand.*

the tropical realist work of Florida painter Jean Welch, whose canvases dominate the living room. Executed in old-master oil technique, many of Welch's pre-Raphaelite images mix a powerful sense of classicism with the surreal.

The exaggerated botanical life so often featured in Welch's work can also be found in abundance in Martinson and Brooke's garden. Martinson considers the two primary influences on the garden to have been the fence, which determined the scale of the landscape, and the paths, which prescribe the experience of movement within it. A canopy of palms, gumbo limbos, baby live oaks, and a dominant royal poinciana tree shelter several varieties of ginger, heliconia, and numerous philodendra and aroids. As part of the garden's low-maintenance design, all of the existing grass was replaced with a ground cover of giant ferns. The only plants in the garden that require periodic tending are orchids and bromeliads, which flourish in Miami's climate.

Fallen royal poinciana blossoms blanket the paths, deck, and ferns in the garden, OPPOSITE. *An oncidium orchid clings to the trunk of a poinciana,* LEFT. *Because the bedrooms are small, the yard beyond their sliding glass doors,* BELOW, *has been intensely planted to extend visual interest.*

This classic urban courtyard serves as an outdoor living room. The house, RIGHT, was designed by Princeton-trained architect Marion Syms Wyeth, who claimed to be Miami's "first educated architect."

tHE MIAMI ARCHITECT ELIZABETH Plater-Zyberk's house in the Dutch/South African village, the last of George Merrick's Coral Gables compounds, reminds her, curiously enough, of the old farmhouses in Pennsylvania where she grew up. Despite the farfetched origins of the design, she finds it appropriate for Miami and for the era in which it was constructed. "This house was built in 1926," she explains, "in what you could call Miami's co-

Clear and Simple

lonial period, a time when establishing the culture was more critical than its refinement. Like so many of those old Pennsylvania farmhouses, our house is an especially graceful, clearly organized building that doesn't rely on details."

Plater-Zyberk and her husband, architect Andres Duany, acquired the two-bedroom house with its enclosed courtyard and detached garage apartment in 1977 from its original owner, Miami's first woman doctor, Hazel Andrews.

In essentially fine condition despite its age, the house required little work for comfort's sake: the architects painted the woodwork white, sandblasted the cathedral ceiling of Dade County pine, added French doors that open out onto the patio, and updated the kitchen.

Plater-Zyberk considers the living room the focus of the house. It lies on an axis with the courtyard, is visible from the dining room, and is also exquisitely scaled. "I make a point of walking through the living room every day, even if I don't have time to sit in it," she says. When the windows in the dining room and living room and the French doors are open, the strong cross-ventilation, enhanced by the tall ceilings, keeps the house cool. Only the bedrooms upstairs are air-conditioned, and only during the dry summers, when no rain releases the heat from the masonry walls.

The couple chose Stickley tables and chairs, furnishings more associated with the Midwest than the South, to reflect the "honest design" of the house: "They're comfortable and tough with no superfluous decoration. They rely on their materials and their design to be what they are." The living room table, for example,

is pegged, not nailed. The chairs are large and comfortable, and all the pieces are solid oak.

Known for their innovative city planning, most notably the town of Seaside, Florida, as well as for their architecture, Duany and Plater-Zyberk feel as much professional respect for their house as they do personal affection. "We really admire it," says Duany. "We strive to do things in our work that are as clear and simple as this house."

Walls, ABOVE AND LEFT, *are finished in an easy-to-apply plaster. The fireplace,* OPPOSITE, *was precast. The living-room table, designed by Gustav Stickley, has a flip top that turns it into a card table.*

dEBRA LYNN YATES AND RAYMOND Jungles believe that even an unfinished house should appear inviting. Like many first-time homeowners, the couple has big plans, a small budget, and a future of many years of living in a work-in-progress. Neither is willing to forfeit the expression of personality because of economic or other limitations. Their recently purchased, architecturally bland suburban ranch house, built in the early 1950s, has put their philosophy to the ultimate test. Jungles, a landscape architect, envisions a day when they can afford to knock out walls for expansive windows and to add garden rooms. Yates, an artist and a design consultant, foresees a spacious master suite opening onto a tropical vista and a maid's room in the children's wing. For the time being, though, they rely on color and artistic invention to imbue their home with a feeling of freshness and ease.

By using pale turquoise and gray on interior walls, they established a sense of rhythm from

A Sense of Color

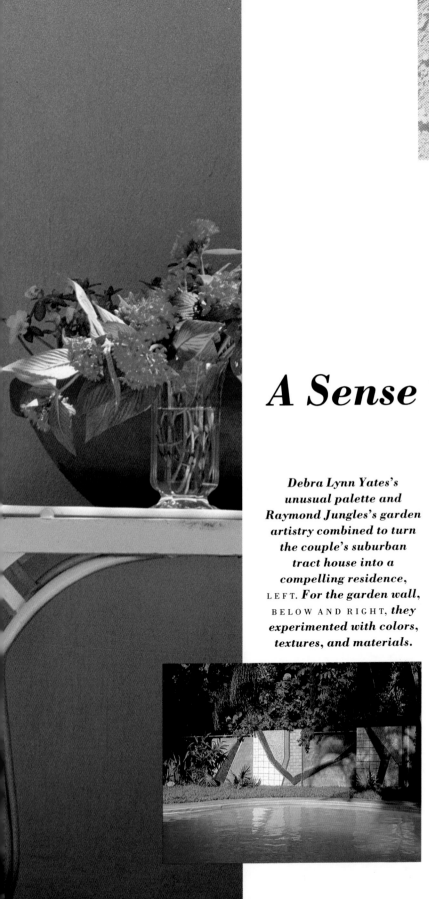

Debra Lynn Yates's unusual palette and Raymond Jungles's garden artistry combined to turn the couple's suburban tract house into a compelling residence, LEFT. *For the garden wall,* BELOW AND RIGHT, *they experimented with colors, textures, and materials.*

one room to the next. "Color is such an easy way to add character," explains Debra Lynn. "You can think about it, experiment with it, play with it wherever you want, and if you don't like what you get, you just paint over it. So many people are afraid to have anything on their walls but white. Here we use white as an accent." Large paintings by Yates and by world-renowned Brazilian landscape architect Roberto Burle Marx, the couple's close friend and mentor, punctuate the walls with additional color and abstract imagery.

One of Yates's passions—and her design trademark—is reworking old furniture. Haunting thrift shops and garage sales, she chooses objects for their shapes and repaints and re-covers to create versatile surfaces. The ovoid table in the living room, for example, was originally bare mahogany with a burgundy leather inset. Twenty or thirty coats of white paint later, it's the ideal complement for the rattan sofa that has been stripped and re-upholstered since it served as a porch couch in their previous home. "Everything here has been given a second life," they agree.

In her furniture arrangements as in her art-

Yates's passion for chairs is in evidence inside, TOP AND ABOVE, *and out,* OPPOSITE, *where oversize foliage surrounds two casually placed formal garden chairs.*

work, Yates uses a free hand. "Just moving things from room to room or rehanging paintings makes a big difference." Her version of Miami style epitomizes casual comfort: for example, she recommends coffee tables that can double as extra seating and couches with loosely upholstered cushions that encourage slouching. The look of her interiors harkens to the days of early Florida, a more somnolent era before the advent of air-conditioning, when it was too hot to hurry.

An Adirondack chair fits comfortably among the Florida room furnishings, OPPOSITE. *The rattan furniture in the living room,* RIGHT AND BELOW, *was dipped, stripped, and waxed, then upholstered loosely to preserve its appealing worn look. Yates gave secondhand wooden chairs,* LEFT AND ABOVE, *her trademark repainting.*

A clutch of ripe coconuts serves as a graphic centerpiece.

*a*S BOATBUILDERS OF SCANDINAVIAN heritage, Avanell and Mel Shoar prize economy and efficiency. For their retirement home, they wanted a highly functional and easily maintained house that would take the greatest possible advantage of its waterfront location. The architect Suzanne Martinson, who grew up in Miami, produced this forcefully expressed Modernist interpretation of a tropical house. So coherent is her elegant response to the

Tropical Modernism

challenges of the subtropical climate that the Shoars feel as at home in this house as they do on one of their own boats.

By devoting the upper floor to the living room, kitchen, and master bedroom, Martinson maximized ventilation and provided unobstructed views of the adjoining estuary. Sliding glass doors on both sides of the one-room-wide house enable the owners to control the flow of air throughout. "The house is so beautifully ventilated that our skin always feels cool," describes Avanell Shoar. "And when

ABOVE, *The Shoar house takes full advantage of its waterfront setting.*

The owners' frequent sailing trips make their home's ease of maintenance an absolute necessity. No-care materials such as the kitchen tile, OPPOSITE ABOVE, and concrete allow them to lock up and leave without concern. BELOW AND RIGHT is the entry screen. On all floors tiles are turned on angle. In the bedroom, OPPOSITE BELOW, a Finnish modern chair is one of the few furnishings.

for irrigation. Rainwater runs down from the cement tile roof through drainpipes and into the cistern. Martinson also used the roof of the cistern to create a terrace.

The main entrance to the house is a monumental staircase that leads directly into the second-floor living room. Here Martinson sustained a sense of mystery about the entry by designing a black-painted, perforated steel screen that blocks the eye but not the air. "As in Japanese architecture," points out Martinson, "you're given only a glimpse of what you see next."

the doors are fully open, we can enjoy the sounds of the water and birdlife below." To further enhance the outdoor sensibilities of the house, Martinson designed a 5-foot overhang that functions much like a Southern gallery or Hawaiian lanai. The overhang shelters the outdoor breakfast area off the kitchen and the balcony off the master bedroom from both rain and summer sun. "We like to savor the storms," says Mrs. Shoar.

The ground floor houses a guest bedroom, guest bath, storage room, and a wood- and metalworking shop. Extending 15 feet out from the middle of this floor is a 14,000-gallon cistern, which holds water used

The house's interior is as elegantly spartan as the architecture. Organized as a continuous flow of space, the rooms of the upper floor lead from one to the other. The bedroom and living room share a double-sided fireplace, enabling the owners to heat the bedroom while relaxing before the living room hearth. Paddle fans, louvered doors, and classic modern furnishings by several designers contribute to the house's contemporary—and Scandinavian—aesthetic.

A five-foot overhang, LEFT, *provides shade and shelter. The house is designed to permit winter sun to penetrate the interior,* BELOW, *ensuring that rooms are filled with warmth and sunlight year round. The monumental staircase,* RIGHT, *is the entryway to the house.*

tHE HOME OF CESAR TRASOBARES, the director of Miami's Art in Public Places program, and the architect Juan Lezcano is in the area of Little Havana where the first wave of Cuban exiles moved in the late 1950s. Unlike most other successful Cubans, who gravitate to such formal residential neighborhoods of Miami as Coral Gables, Trasobares and Lezcano preferred to settle in a neighborhood where the expatriate culture is still strong and identifiable. The house, built in 1929 as a two-story duplex, reminded Trasobares of the beach house his family once owned in Cuba's Oriente province, an informal, concrete two-story bungalow with a wraparound porch.

Both art director and architect are more interested in process than product, and both prefer nontraditional design to the comforts of the familiar. The process of remodeling their house "evolves intuitively," they say. They have no master plan, no schedule, and no definitive goal. Rather, they see the house as an art project, one that progresses at its own

Refuge in Little Havana

Originally a two-family house, this Little Havana residence has been converted into a combination home-office-gallery by its Cuban-born owners, who chose the neighborhood for its ethnic spirit. Downtown Miami is visible through the multicolored, multi-textured living room window, OPPOSITE. *At the back of the house is a brick terrace,* RIGHT.

pace. "The idea was to create a casual place for both entertaining and working," explains Trasobares. "Even though we might be concentrating on several parts of the house at the same time, we generally allow one idea to lead to the next."

From time to time, they toy with the idea of giving each facade a different treatment, a sort of architectural summary of southern Florida styles: the north would be Florida Conch, a wood structure with a veranda off the kitchen; the west, Mediterranean, with a bougainvillea-covered terrace; the southern face would be a bungalow, mirroring the house next door; and the north, an exposed concrete elevation.

Trasobares and Lezcano designed the garden as if it were another room of the house, building an 8-foot concrete wall around the front, back, and one side. A chain-link fence stretches along the other side against a thick green hedge of aurelias. When they removed the old concrete of the front sidewalk, Lezcano restructured it as a garden path and recycled the shards into a bench and three lanterns.

The house's interior is correspondingly inventive. Ninety percent of its furniture is de-

The sculptural table, TOP, *is one of many pieces of furniture designed by Lezcano and Trasobares. In a wall niche is a sculpture by Carol Brown,* ABOVE. *The living room,* RIGHT, *is filled with wicker furniture and art exhibition posters.*

Framed posters of contemporary artists' exhibitions fill the walls of the downstairs sitting room, INSET ABOVE LEFT, *and the upstairs living room,* ABOVE, *which overlooks the garden. The exposed concrete block in the downstairs sitting room,* LEFT, *enhances natural ventilation and visually connects indoors to outdoors. Lezcano's table in the downstairs sitting room,* OPPOSITE, *echoes the dynamic poster by Keith Haring.*

signed and made by the owners. The lamp hanging over the upstairs dining room table, for example, is a heavy-duty extension cord connected to a Japanese paper lantern; the kitchen shelves are 1 × 8-inch planks suspended from the ceiling on stainless-steel nautical cables; and the awning that shelters the entrance to the house combines canvas, metal pipe, and fence hardware.

With its private living and working spaces upstairs (living room, bedrooms, library, kitchen, and dining room/work area) and public and professional spaces downstairs (Lezcano's studio and an exhibition area in which Trasobare's collection of finger rings is displayed), the home functions like a town house, an urban type appropriate to its owners' Old Havana origins.

Monumental in construction yet picturesque in setting, the garden bench was assembled from concrete shards created when the house's front sidewalk was dug out and replaced.

tHE SARASOTA ARCHITECT CARL ABbott always approaches the design of a house by first thoroughly studying the proposed site. He analyzes the passage of breezes, angles of light, and the direction of its most dynamic and restful views.

Abbott's houses, though often massive in feeling and therefore very grounded, are, in fact, also often multilevel, partly because in Florida's flat landscape, an upper level provides an exciting vantage point. "I try to go up

Uplifted by the View

when it's appropriate," Abbott remarks. "Nevertheless, all my buildings grow from the ground, from a feeling of being very much tied to the earth."

The site of this hardedged, informal residence of dynamic architectural character is an island with a beautiful view of the nearby bay and adjoining 60-acre wildlife preserve. A less imaginative architect might have located the house in the center of the property, with the water on one

Vast spatial proportions amplify the interior, LEFT. *The stuccoed exterior,* INSET ABOVE AND ABOVE, *matches the color of seashells.*

side and the garden on the other. Abbott considers the placement of a home in the middle of a lot a mistake. Instead, he works around the site, along its edges, in order to "look into its beauty." In this case, his clients, who are passionate gardeners, had a specification that reinforced Abbott's thinking: they wanted an uninterrupted vista from the house to the garden and beyond to the bay.

With this in mind, Abbott stretched the house plan along a single axis and sited it so that its three multistory window walls face the adjoining wildlife preserve on the south, the bay on the east, and a beach on the west. Along the north elevation, a solid masonry wall provides privacy and protection from winter winds and conserves energy. A roof deck offers a 360-degree view.

The interior shares this sense of clarity and drama. The three-story, 30-foot-tall entry hall opens onto a suspended upper-level den and then to the high rooftop deck. Living room and dining room are located near the bay, with views to the water and "jungle." Bedrooms and bathrooms are situated in the horizontal wing that looks out onto the garden.

A double-height screened porch overlooks the yard.

Abbott used contrast to enliven the simplicity of the design: a large area of stucco is played against an expanse of glass wall, horizontal next to vertical. The effect of such juxtapositions is that the elements—fragility and massiveness, height and width—amplify one another, harmonize, and generate a feeling of serenity and strength.

The architect prefers to use only a few materials in a house: here, wood, tile, and glass. "Materials alone don't make good architecture," he insists. "It's the way they all work together." He used bleached Western cedar on the balcony and on the columns and cross members of the window walls, and Mexican Saltillo tile for the floors. Classic Mies van der Rohe pieces and English and Oriental antiques furnish the rooms, deliberately left spare to accentuate architectural lines and volumes.

The minimal vocabulary of materials is matched by a similarly limited range of colors. "I treat color less as a means of decorative enhancement and more as a neutral presence against which surrounding nature is dramatized," he explains. "The intention, you see, is to throw you visually right back outside."

The house is situated so that interior spaces, such as the dining room, ABOVE, and outdoor areas, such as the spa, OPPOSITE, take full advantage of the adjoining estuary. Birds can be seen and heard year round.

*t*HE STAINED-GLASS ARTIST BOBBY Bant built her own house from a picture in her mind and with relatively few dollars in her pocket. The picture she had was of a stylish, contemporary, spacious residence: a two-story loft, a marble fireplace, tile floors, a sweeping wall of windows, and an in-

The owner's passion for collecting and bargain hunting served her well in the furnishing and landscaping of her built-from-scratch house. The Art Deco-era bust and vase, LEFT, and the grand piano, RIGHT, were purchased at minimal prices. Plantings from cuttings and yard sales fill the garden, BELOW RIGHT.

door reflecting pool. Consulting with the architect Alex Sturman on design, she bought most of the materials and fixtures at close-outs,

Modern Masterpiece

turned up furniture at garage sales or designed and built it herself, and even did some of the construction. "I was the contractor, truck

driver, glass-block builder, steel layer, and eventually even drywall finisher," she proudly relates.

Bant's 3,000-square-foot house, located in a ½-acre pine woods, combines clever calculation with imagination. To capture the maxi-

mum amount of north light, she built a two-story wall of sliding glass doors facing the pool side. When the hot, humid summer and mosquito-laden rainy season come to an end, the entire side of the house is opened to transform the living room into a giant cabana.

The white 12-inch-square floor tiles, cool on the feet and to the eye, and the gray marble fireplace reinforce the austerity of the interior black, white, and gray color scheme. Only the hot pink wall behind the mantel and the blue water of the pool are reminiscent of Miami's traditional hues.

Inspired by the contemporary designer Gae Aulenti, Bant built a cocktail-table-on-casters. She also designed the poolside dining table, using a commercial display case as a base. Opposite the dining area she left the kitchen

Bant found the marble for the fireplace and Italian tile for the floors, ABOVE, *at closeout sales. The glass block divider,* BELOW RIGHT, *separates the kitchen from the living room without closing out light or view. In the kitchen,* OPPOSITE, *colorful counter tiles mix with a vivid collection of Fiestaware pitchers.*

exposed, partly in order to display her spectacular 450-piece collection of Fiestaware. Glass-
fronted cabinets and open shelving keep her
cookware and equipment either in view or
within reach; even the food is housed in an old,
glass-door refrigerator.

Throughout the house glass block gives the
look and feel of coolness and has the additional
advantage of being easy to maintain. For Bant
its appeal is its ability to provide both light and
privacy, and to set off her Fiestaware collection. Glass block and Fiestaware, highlights of
industrial design, give the house its echoes of
the interiors of the 1940s.

*The indoor/outdoor
pool was at the head of
Bant's wish list; it gives
an almost Hollywood touch
to the carefully
considered interior.
The pool flows under the
window wall from table-
side to screened patio.*

"THE BEACH THEME HAS ALWAYS RUN through my playtime," explains Babette Herschberger, whose affinity for sun, fun, and sand brought her from Indiana to the Miami Beach Art Deco district. She chose the neighborhood for its colorful style and proximity to the ocean, and her apartment building for its lawn. A frangipani tree—the Hawaiian tree from which leis are made—grows just outside her window in the courtyard.

A fan of 1930s and 1940s diners, Herschber-

By the Sea, by the Sea

ger copied their motifs in her apartment. A neon sign she carried as hand luggage on a plane from Oregon decorates the living room wall, and a big, bold black-and-white checkerboard pattern predominates in upholstery, shower curtain, and towels.

Babette Herschberger's Miami Beach Art Deco district apartment, seen from the courtyard, ABOVE AND RIGHT, *fulfilled her dreams of a tropical playground. She decorated it with garage sale finds, such as the framed photographs on the mantel,* LEFT. *The photograph in the circular frame is of her grandfather.*

The floor in front of the faux fireplace, which Herschberger created from broken black and white tiles and gray cement, echoes the checkerboard theme.

Bold checkerboard fabric gives graphic definition to the living room, ABOVE. *Herschberger laid the mosaic tile flooring,* OPPOSITE AND RIGHT, *herself. A neon sign,* TOP, *highlights the period resort atmosphere.*

Outdoor chairs, another of Herschberger's beach-theme passions, are the principal furnishing of the one-bedroom home. A slatted Adirondack-style chair is painted to match her seafoam green walls, and a diminutive wicker beach chair from China, which she found in Key West, not only folds—as good portable recreational furniture should—but is also equipped to store magazines. The seaside dominates everywhere, creating a relaxed, updated version of Miami Beach living.

The repetition of the living room's checkerboard pattern in the bathroom, OPPOSITE, *is an example of Herschberger's sense of whimsy. Postcards and framed palms,* ABOVE AND RIGHT, *underscore the tropical theme. Although the creamy pastel color of Herschberger's walls is known as seafoam, her friends refer to it as "toothpaste green."*

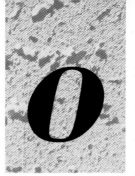

ONE OF THE MOST WIDELY PHOTO-graphed houses in America, the Pink House, as it has come to be known, is a breezy suburban residence made dramatic not only by its bold hue but also by a powerful balance of form, light, and scale. Designed by Laurinda Spear and Bernardo Fort-Brescia of the ground-breaking firm Arquitectonica International for Spear's parents, its color statement received international attention in the late 1970s. Although the press was impressed, neighbors were so disturbed by the house's three-planed red, rose, and pink street-facing wall that they appealed to a local design review board to demand that a grove of trees be planted to shield the house

The Pink House

from the street. Nowadays the Spear house has transcended the shock of the new. Narrow and tall on its double-width lot, it takes maximum advantage of its bay frontage, its east facade facing Biscayne Bay and Miami Beach beyond. The main living areas—library, living room, dining room, and kitchen —are organized *en suite* on the ground floor, each with windows that frame the view to the

Unlike its suburban neighbors, the Spears's house has no lawn, but rather a carpet of concrete pavers that echo the rigid geometry of window grids and glass blocks on the back facade, ABOVE. *The porthole window,* OPPOSITE, *derives from Miami's Art Deco heritage, which in turn drew inspiration from ocean liners.*

water in a different way. A main corridor, 4½ feet wide, 18 feet high, and more than 100 feet long runs parallel to this series of rooms and is punctuated with windows that open onto the west-facing pool deck. Two bedrooms, two dressing rooms, and two studies occupy the upper stories, where they receive the breezes and light from both east and west. A tall bay-front porch offers sunshine at breakfast and shade in the afternoon.

Stark and modern as the exterior of the house appears, its interior features traditional rooms and understated décor. White walls focus attention on the architecture; tile floors reinforce the aura of cool austerity.

Despite its postmodern genre, the Pink House pays homage to Miami's design past in its stuccoed concrete-block construction, pool porthole, canopied deck, and the glorious row of royal palms that are as identifiably tropical as the once-shocking Caribbean pink.

The windows, ABOVE, *are closed only during the height of summer, when air conditioning is used. The narrow residence is so well ventilated that breezes keep the house cool for most of the year. The grand piano,* LEFT, *takes on a sculptural monumentality in the sparsely furnished living room.*

The 60-x-12 foot pool, RIGHT, *lies between the house itself and the glass block and stucco wall in front. Completely enclosed and private, the patio,* ABOVE AND OPPOSITE, *serves as an outdoor salon. The shiplike railings,* OPPOSITE, *are reminiscent of those used in early Miami Beach hotels.*

R **D** **E** **N**

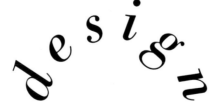

*m*iami, unlike most of the continental United States, which is temperate in climate, is in the subtropical zone, and its growing season is the reverse of that in most of the rest of the country. In spring, while Northern and Western homeowners are sowing their *design* annuals, Miamians are raking up avocado, mango, and sea grape leaves. And in fall, when others are harvesting,

173

gardeners in southern Florida begin to plant. It is understandable that newcomers to Miami are often confounded by the garden.

Two sounds distinguish the city's aural landscape: the roar of lawn mowers and the steady hum of air conditioners. Ignoring the climate, most Miami homeowners have sodded their property with grass, and while they are outside attempting to dominate the subtropical life force with bimonthly cutting, the rest of the population is inside, seeking refrigerated refuge from the heat and humidity.

Although the weather, the mosquitoes, and the shallow, rocky alkaline soil easily daunt many residents, others have proved that gardening can be a source of creative excitement. In fact, few regions of this country offer Miami's luxury of year-round outdoor indulgence and garden cultivation. Landscape devices, such as vine-covered pergolas, offer shelter from strong summer sun. Tall shade trees, such as poincianas, jacarandas, and ficus, provide comfortable natural canopies.

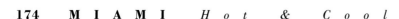

Ferns, liriope, wedelia, lantana, and even mulch, used as ground cover in place of grass, permit homeowners to elude constant mowing. Fountains offer the restful coolness of water, and tree-lined allées encourage breezes.

One increasingly critical factor in the planning of southern Florida gardens is the availability of water. As the Biscayne aquifer, the table of fresh water just below the peninsula, diminishes, the importance of using native plants, such as coco plum, myrtle of the river, sea grape, and buttonwood (both silver and green), which are far less thirsty than exotics, increases. In addition, native flora, which are also resistant to most subtropical insects and diseases because they have adapted to the climatic conditions, do not require fertilizer.

Just as Miami's architecture is characterized by a few distinct styles, so is the garden design of its various neighborhoods. Coconut Grove, a village settled by bohemians and pioneers who discarded the boundaries of their

established worlds, has the city's most untamed landscape, that of a natural hammock. In this casual community, it is hard to tell where one property starts and another stops, projecting the illusion as you drive its shady, winding streets that what you see is a wood that belongs to everyone.

The Bahamians who, in the late 1800s, were among the Grove's first residents, were said to arrive "with a pocket full of seeds." Protected from the salt air by its thick foliage and with a microclimate that encouraged healthy growth, the Grove's botanical bounty flourished, embellished by  the lemons, velvet apples, loquats, and other exotic fruit trees imported by the Caribbean settlers. In fact, it is from these trees that much of Miami's early planting derived. Often, enterprising gardeners or homeowners would drive around the Grove, spot an interesting tree, and ask its owner for a cutting.

As natural and unrestrained as is Coconut Grove's landscape, so studiously planned is Coral Gables', an approach that is in keeping with the formal quality of the neighborhood's Mediterranean architecture. Like all of Miami, Coral Gables originally hosted little more vegetation than slash pine and scrub palmetto. But by the 1940s, aurelia, hibiscus, and ficus hedges had come to delineate ownership of its picturesque lots where open, grassy lawns were regularly manicured. Hundreds of live oak trees planted along Coral Way by the Civilian Conservation Corps (CCC) before World War II matured into a picturesque allée, creating one of the Gables' most seductive boulevards.

Pines, palms, and vines characterize the landscape of Miami Beach where, despite softer, less rocky soil, the garden palette is limited by the salt content of the air. In the 1970s, a blight called Lethal Yellowing killed nearly all the region's coconut palms, the tree most identified with Miami's picture-postcard image. Today, blight-resistant Malayan palms have replaced the earlier coconuts.

HE ART COLLECTOR AND BENEFACtor Mitchell Wolfson, Jr., had the good fortune to grow up not only in a house of stately character, but in a landscape where personal inventiveness was combined with a Mediterranean-like beauty. He had the further good fortune to later own this childhood house and garden.

Wolfson's family moved into the Italian-style villa in 1947, when the sixth-generation Floridian was eight years old. In 1983, after years of schooling, traveling, and a diplomatic career, Wolfson, who also owns a 300-year-old restored *rustico* in Genoa, Italy, purchased the Miami Beach residence from his family's estate to provide him with both a connection to his deep community roots and a stateside pied à terre.

Mediterranean Retreat

A bonsaied banyan tree, ABOVE, *announces the entry to the bayside Wolfson estate,* TOP. *Wrought-iron furniture and grilles distinguish the courtyard,* OPPOSITE AND BELOW RIGHT.

Built in 1937 for the Bohn family of the Bohn Brass and Bronze Company, the estate is filled with examples of metal detailing by artists Paul Manship and Samuel Yellin, two of the finest metalcrafters of the era. The Art Deco medallions on the

The courtyard and loggia, OPPOSITE, *are punctuated by Roman arches. The loggia's floor is paved with Spanish tiles, and the original decorative stenciling is still visible on its pine-beam ceiling. Ginger thrives in a mosaic tile planter,* BELOW AND RIGHT. *The medallions on the entry grille,* BELOW RIGHT, *were designed by Paul Manship, one of the United States' most highly regarded metal sculptors.*

183

entry grille, for example, designed by Manship, add a pictorial quality to the landscape architecture, which, like the house, combines the deep tones of a Venetian Deco palette.

The east-facing front entry court provides a picturesque setting for outdoor entertaining and relaxation. To the left of this tropical piazza lies a rose garden framed by jasmine hedges, banana trees, and Florida cypress.

An elegant loggia, surrounding the entry garden on two sides, is articulated by Roman arches and constructed of materials chosen for their durability and beauty: the ceilings are supported by beams of Dade County pine (their original decorative stenciling is still visible), and the floors are paved with classic Spanish tiles and cool, tinted terrazzo.

An accomplished Chinese landscape painter, Wolfson's mother, Frances, had the massive banyan trees at the entrance pruned in bonsai fashion, a process that required decades of precise and informed labor. The effect is both dramatic and monumental.

The tile in the fountain, surrounded by an ixora hedge and lilies, dates from the 1920s, OPPOSITE. *Bahamian shutters,* INSET RIGHT, *shield the house from the westerly sun. The molded column,* HERE, *is made of concrete overlaid with stucco, a common Miami combination of building materials.*

The landscape of the garden varies from lush density to calm vistas such as that of Royal Palm Lake. ABOVE RIGHT, Coville's glory flowers only in October, and, ABOVE FAR RIGHT, a royal poinciana blooms in early summer.

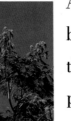

*t*HE FAIRCHILD TROPICAL GARDEN, located along Miami's historic, winding Old Cutler Road, is the largest tropical botanical garden in the continental United States. Named after David Fairchild, the first chief of plant exploration for the U.S. Department of Agriculture (he brought back from around the world thousands of edible and ornamental plants that influenced agriculture and changed the American diet), it contains over more than six thousand plants, among them some of the world's finest collections—in both quantity and qual-

World-Class Wonder

ity—of palms, cycads, tropical flowering plants, aroids, ferns, Bahamian plants, bromeliads, and orchids.

The Garden was founded in 1938 by Colonel Robert H. Montgomery, a New York tax accountant, self-made millionaire, and avid gardener whose passion was the growing of palms and cycads. In time, his plant collection outgrew his private estate and the colonel began looking for a way to make it accessible to the public. Learning that David Fairchild had retired here, he approached the famed horticulturist and together the two began working on plans for Montgomery's 83-acre gift to Miami.

To design the site, Montgomery hired William Lyman Phillips, a landscape architect who had begun his career in the Boston offices of the famed Frederick Law Olmstead, designer of New York's Central Park, Prospect Park, Forest Hills, and scores of other outstanding landscapes throughout America. Phillips, who had visited botanical gardens throughout Europe, had come to Florida to design the Bok Tower Gardens near Lakeland and was working on Matheson Hammock Park, adjacent to the Fairchild site, when he met Montgomery.

In full appreciation of Montgomery's and Fairchild's desires, Phillips designed a garden filled with lush variety. It features eleven lakes, two dramatic vistas, a 25-acre palmetum, and paths that wind through a tropical rain forest, a fern glade, a rock and cactus garden, and a hibiscus garden. He also in-

Vibrant bougainvillea blooms year round, TOP. *From the luxuriant shelter of the Bailey Palm Glade,* ABOVE, *one comes suddenly upon the wide expanse of Pandanus Lake,* OPPOSITE, *which is framed by the characteristic stiltlike roots of pandani.*

cluded a flowering vine pergola, a cycad circle, a sunken garden, and a rare plant house.

Phillips contrasted compact, informally grouped masses of plants with wide lawns and expansive vistas, producing the effect of ever-changing scale and anticipation. For plants indigenous to southern Florida, the Florida Keys, and the Bahamas, he created areas that simulate their native habitats. In other sections, plants and trees that were endangered in their native environments, such as the bottle palm from the Mascarene Islands in the Indian Ocean and the *Microcycas calocoma*, a Cuban cycad, flourish. Endangered Florida species such as the buccaneer palm from the Florida Keys and the royal palm are also preserved here.

Orchids, bromeliads, giant tree ferns, and other exotic plants are on perpetual display in the garden's rare plant house. And flowering plants of one kind or another, such as hibiscus, red silk-cotton trees, and bougainvillea vines, are in bloom throughout the year. Regardless of the season, Fairchild Tropical Garden is resplendent.

The rare plant house, ABOVE, *shelters hundreds of types of exotic flora.* RIGHT, *royal palms visible from the gardens' original coral rock wall. The small pool in the Bailey Palm Glade,* OPPOSITE, *is home to Fairchild's occasional visiting alligators.*

a STAND OF LIVE OAKS, PRUNED AND trained for decades into a towering canopy, dramatizes this romantic garden owned by former mayor of Miami Maurice Ferre and his wife, Mercedes. So enamored were the Ferres with the splendor of this grove that they named their residence "Hioaks." "The oak trees were the focus for everything done here," states Ferre. "Their massive canopy and its exquisite filtering of light are the heart of this garden."

The trees were planted long before the original Tudor-style cottage, located behind the main house, was built more than sixty years ago, making them older than most trees in Miami. The continuous shade they provide, which inhibits the growth of grass, and the moisture they retain at ground level turn the surrounding area into a virtual hothouse, perfect for the growth of ferns, orchids, and bromeliads. Even the house's oak-covered, shake-shingle roof supports a colony of ferns.

Hioaks

Former Miami mayor Maurice Ferre and his wife, Mercedes, live in an English-style house surrounded by a Spanish-style wall set in a subtropical garden. The carved wooden entry gates were made in Gerona, Spain.

The Ferres have cultivated a Mediterranean-landscape feeling in their garden. Using the nearby Villa Vizcaya as a reference, they mixed umbria and sienna to reproduce the yellow of its surrounding wall in their own garden. They next had the wall stained with a lime-based paint that develops a patina with age and rain. "The older it gets, the nicer it looks," comments Ferre.

The Ferres have a large family and an extensive social calendar, so they particularly enjoy entertaining in the garden. Planted informally but organized with care for details, it is divided into separate areas for lounging, dining, breakfasting, and socializing. Remarkably, all these enclaves are within view of one another, giving the garden a sense of uninterrupted vista.

A classical obelisk, found in San Miguel de Allende, Mexico, stands at one end of a blue-tiled reflecting pool that lies perpendicular to massive, carved wood entry doors, made in Spain. Other classical garden ornaments—carved stone fountains, urns, and reflecting balls atop pedestals—add grace and a hint of formality to the lyrical tumult of foliage.

The shade, filtered light, and moist environment fostered by live oak trees more than sixty years old— rare antiquity in a young city like Miami—provide an ideal environment for ferns and bromeliads. In addition, the garden has more than twenty-four varieties of palms.

PRIVATE BUT NEVER IMPENETRABLE, this sprawling palmetum was begun in 1975 when its owner adopted the deserted land adjoining his home and began to cultivate a personally styled jungle. "There was nothing here but an interesting topography and two strange columns," he explains. "I was instantly enticed by these elements."

Considering flowers too fussy and delicate

Botanical Profusion

for the vigorous climate of southern Florida, he opted for a bold landscape of foliage and trees. Massed to form canopies and coves, more than a hundred varieties of palms form the heart of the garden. "Some people like to set palms out as individual pieces, but if your taste runs toward a jungle effect, you can't have them sitting like statues. What's more, the palms are always changing—there's great competition for survival—and I prefer that dynamic of

Fifteen years ago, this dense palmetum was a forest of Australian pines. Now more than one hundred different palm varieties flourish here. To give the garden an underlying harmony, curves are balanced with angularity and sun with shade. Meandering paths provide mystery.

growth to pure decorativeness. With this approach, I have a garden I can change at will."

And transform it he does often, without a formal scheme or plan. Some trees have been moved as many as four times to accommodate the vista or path or backdrop effect he is creating at the moment. Testimony to these native plants' hardiness, only a few have failed to reroot successfully.

Besides its density, the garden's most outstanding feature is its changes of elevation, highly unusual terrain for flat Miami. Although a natural ridge runs through the property, the owner enhanced the contrasts in height by banking cuttings, dirt, and sand to create berms or mounds. Amplifying this drama, paths that wind, bend, and dip through the foliage provide the garden with an unending sense of mystery.

Changes in elevation create a dramatic setting for outdoor dining, OPPOSITE. *Carved-stone garden ornaments,* ABOVE, BELOW LEFT, AND RIGHT, *offer contrast to the setting's intense green.*

The stuccoed facade combines texture and Caribbean color. A concrete entry arch, OPPOSITE, directs the way through a gridded carpet of grass and concrete pavers to the two-story studio.

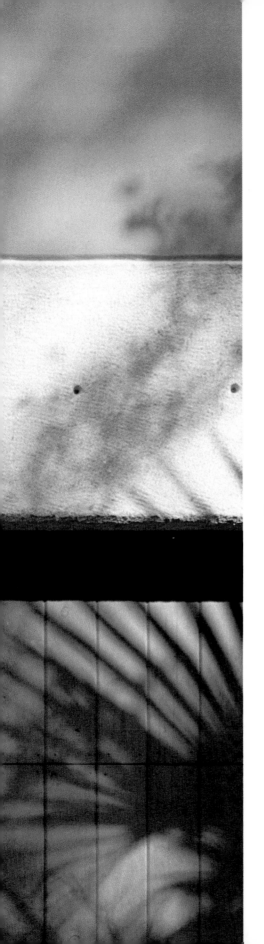

SO QUIET AND SECLUDED IS THIS SUBurban estate that even its pines and oaks seem to shy from notice. Yet one element dramatically announces presence: a grand entry arch that states that this is not just another ranch house.

The arch directs the way to a small, two-story stucco home, tidily composed to contain two single-car garages below and a guest room and artist's studio above. It is the first installment of a residential compound

Simple Compound

plan designed by the architect Daniel Williams for Gabriele and Patrick Fiorentino. Still in planning are a 3,500-square-foot house to be connected to the guest house/studio by a 40-foot-long bridge.

A forty-year-old house stood on the property when the Fiorentinos purchased it, but they were more interested in a contemporary residence. They considered a number of plans, including a house they could build in stages, until Williams suggested the compound idea.

Everything about this modest initial struc-

ture is provocative and deft. It is posed on the site in a way that completes the sense of arrival anticipated by the entry arch. Proportions are simple and the stucco cladding adds texture without detracting from the clean architectural lines.

The upper story is reached by a stairway of cut keystone that ascends the side of the building at a 270-degree angle. Mindful of Miami's 65-inch-a-year average rainfall, Williams copied an architectural device of the Romans and positioned the staircase a fraction of an inch away from the wall to allow rainwater to run alongside rather than over the tops of the steps.

Inside, a skylight and westward-facing windows brighten the guest room and studio. Compact yet open to the elements, these quarters resemble a tree house with a ship's galley.

A second-story walkway functions as an elevated garden path, ABOVE LEFT AND LEFT. *The house's paint actually floats on the surface of the stucco,* OPPOSITE.

*a*MONG THE MOST CURIOUS, BEAUTIful, and fanciful of George Merrick's international compounds is the Chinese Village, a block of eight houses designed by Henry Killam Murphy, the New York architect and authority on Chinese architecture. Like the Peking residences of the Ming dynasty, after which they were modeled, Murphy's square- and U-shaped Gables houses have entry courts and inner courtyards; and, like courtyard houses everywhere, were designed specifically to provide privacy in urban settings. The Chinese

Oriental Fantasy

Village houses are especially well suited to Miami's warm, humid climate with their cross-ventilated interiors and thick insulating walls. Common rooms, which open into gardens or courtyards, simultaneously function as indoor and outdoor spaces. High surrounding walls diminish noise.

Marlene Weiss, an architectural designer, and her husband, the developer

Henry Killam Murphy drew on the Chinese traditions of bright-colored roof tiles, curved roof corners, garden walls, ornate garden gates, and detailed woodwork in his design of this Coral Gables house.

Rick Mattaway, moved into their Chinese Village home, built in 1923 as the compound's sales model, in 1978. Though they were thrilled at the way the property's zero lot line afforded the long, narrow 50-foot-by-175-foot garden ample room for landscape, they were dismayed at the garden's overall condition. "What we had was an open yard with no wall, no fence, a 60-year-old ixora hedge that had grown itself out, and a nonfunctioning fish pond that looked like a compost heap," describes Mattaway. They turned to landscape architect Leonardo Alvarez, who devised a plan that combines English picturesqueness with the contemplative aura of a classic Oriental garden. A keystone walkway that reaches from the porch door through a cluster of dwarf bougainvillea, as well as a variety of spatial experiences, invites romantic strolling. Boulders and granite chips (which change color as the weather changes—white when dry, dark when wet) are surrounded by a carpet of zoysia grass and form a quiet, spare composition reminiscent of the Japanese Zen gardens of raked gravel.

Seventy-five percent of the plants in the present garden were already growing on the property. Alvarez relocated most for visual and horticultural advantage and then added others, such as bamboo, dwarf heliconia, *Rhapis* palms, and Alexander palms, for character and beauty. Both Alvarez and the homeowners agonized over the removal of a mature mango tree, which, though it gave delicious fruit, was too large for the scale of the garden. They replaced it with a delicate, yellow-blooming cassia tree that flowers year round and is the colorful focal point of the garden.

A teakwood garden bench lends a picturesque English flavor to the Weiss/ Mattaway garden in which more than twelve different varieties of palms grow.

A screened porch off the living room, added in the 1930s, was given a painted lintel detail that relates to the house's Chinese motif, ABOVE. *The antique wicker tea cart,* LEFT, *was a gift from the couple's mother.*

The shadowy guest garden features a cooling fountain. ABOVE, *the pool garden invites strolling as well as sunning. A frieze in the guest garden,* TOP RIGHT, *depicts an exotic oasis. The rhythmic verticality of a traveler's palm and palm trunk are accentuated by a wrought iron grille,* RIGHT.

*g*RAND IN SCALE BUT NOT OVERLY DE-signed, this southern Florida garden combines an untamed tropicality with classical restraint. Little more than a glance from the Atlantic Ocean, it is above all a garden for strolling and repose, exactly the indulgences desired by its Northern owners, who enjoy it as a retreat.

A Garden for Meandering

Composed like a triptych, the landscape surrounding the Spanish Mediterranean–style house built in 1929 incorporates three distinct gardens that lie parallel to each other and to the nearby beachfront. The dominant middle garden, which focuses on a rectangular pool, is the most architectural in design, with walls, tiled walkways, a monumental gate, and a pool house. To the east, toward the Atlantic, lies

the "wilderness" garden in a gully through which a stream once ran. Here a small forest of native plants

Stucco walls and barrel-tile roofs define the Mediterranean character of the garden setting, ABOVE AND OPPOSITE. *The gate,* TOP, *leads to the wilderness garden.*

now flourishes. To the west is the "guest" garden, the most lavishly planted and intimate of the three.

The middle garden, designed to function as an outdoor living room, is carefully proportioned, yet casual in tone. Enclosed by a low Australian pine hedge on one side, it faces the pool house and cabana on the other. At the terminus stands a stone-and-metal gate that was added several years ago. Originally, the owners had planned to build a wall across the garden's southern end to increase their privacy, but they realized that it would truncate the long vista and obstruct the view of a sculptural fountain.

Instead, they turned to New York architect Alex Gorlin, who suggested a gate that would enclose the garden without hiding the view of the fountain. Based on the baroque Porta Pia gateway in Genoa, Italy, the gate reflects the setting's Mediterranean feeling. Rusticated columns contrast with whimsical scrollwork, which evokes ocean waves.

In contrast to the formal garden, the wilderness garden is a dramatic tangle of shapes and shadows. Over the last few years, the land-

The scrolls and stylized wave pattern of the monumental gate designed by architect Alex Gorlin, ABOVE AND RIGHT, *are based on the baroque Porta Pia gateway in Genoa, Italy. The loggia,* BELOW AND OPPOSITE, *offers a sun-sheltered spot for entertaining.*

scape architect Helen Eelhart has gouged a jungle path through what had become an impenetrable grove in the dry steambed that runs alongside a column of lacy Australian pines. She filled the basin with egg rock, pruned and nourished the existing sea grapes, and added coarse-textured tropical plants, such as philodendron, Spanish bayonet, croton, and traveler's palm, as well as hearty flowering trees such as jacaranda, Hong Kong orchid, and hibiscus. "My palette was limited because of the effects of salt air," she explains. "Fortunately, my clients favor the garden's native appeal and enjoy the contrast between the wild and the cultivated."

Picturesque and secluded, the guest garden is bisected by the guest wing and garage. Bark-covered paths lead to a shaded bench on the north side, and on the south a keystone walkway leads to a sculptural fountain framed by royal palms. Here also citrus and avocado trees flourish under a canopy of mature live oaks to create shaded nooks.

The stylistic variety of the gardens gives the landscape an aura of unpredictability: it is a retreat designed for gentle surprise.

The three-acre Flamingo Lake, ABOVE AND OPPOSITE, *was developed forty years ago. A Florida alligator sleeps on a bed of coral rock,* BELOW. *The Parrot Jungle sign,* RIGHT, *has welcomed visitors for more than fifty years.*

d REAMY-LOOKING AS A 1940S ROMANtic comedy and happy as a 1950s summer vacation, Parrot Jungle is all Technicolor and exaggeration. With its feathers, flowers, colors, vistas, 40-foot-high palms, and 15-foot-long alligators, this 12-acre garden attraction could well have been Busby Berkeley's vision of paradise. So lush and exotic is the setting, in fact, that it is easy to imagine Dorothy Lamour posing languidly in a sarong among its extravagant flora. More than 1,100 birds (75 species of parrots, cranes, macaws, geese, peafowl, native ibis, swans, exotic ducks, spoonbills, cockatiels, cockatoos, parakeets, lovebirds, crowned pigeons, peacocks, and the famous flock of over 80 flamingoes) live here among 100 different varieties of cactus and succulents and 2,000 varieties of tropical and subtropical plants and trees.

Originally a 20-acre cypress and oak hammock, the garden was started in the late 1930s by Austrian-born Franz Scherr. With $5,000 from the mortgage of his home, he purchased

Snapshot Paradise

the land, hired a crew to help him clear trails, erected a pine entryway with a thatched roof (today faced with coral rock and used as the juice bar), and opened the attraction with six macaws, an alligator, a rattlesnake, a deodorized skunk, and a bunch of raccoons. The first year, 10,000 tourists paid 25¢ each to walk through the swampy setting. Today, approximately 300,000 people a year wander the wonderland, observe bird-training sessions, attend the trained-parrot shows in the amphitheater, and pose for snapshots with the birds.

For the last forty-eight years, Parrot Jungle has specialized in propagating bright multicolored macaws. Every morning twenty-five pairs are released to fly freely around Miami. At night, called by name, they return home.

The garden, though informally planned, offers a vast horticultural variety. Its plantings range from water-loving examples such as heliconia and other gingers to high-ground plants that need good drainage, such as hibiscus and crotons; from plants that require full sun, such as bougainvillea and flame vine, to those that thrive in complete shade, such as orchids.

An African crown crane roams freely on the grounds, ABOVE.

The Desert Garden, BELOW, *was planted in the 1950s. It contains more than two hundred varieties of cactus and succulents.*

The macaws, LEFT, *fifty of which fly freely around Miami, are bred and fed at Parrot Jungle and never fail to return home each night.*

ABOVE, *canna lilies, yellow and green crotons, and a climbing aroid fill a corner of the Jungle Garden.*

LEFT, *cactus and succulents are topped by a vivid bougainvillea in the Desert Garden. Water lilies,* RIGHT, *surround cypress knees.*

miami—*beach capital and tropical paradise—is as much a state of mind as it is a center of attention. This guide offers sources for creating a little Miami anywhere and suggestions for visiting sources of inspiration in Miami and a few miles down the road.*

Antiques

ALHAMBRA ANTIQUES CENTER
3640 Coral Way
Miami, Fla. 33145
(305) 446-1688
Furniture accessories and collectibles. Twenty dealers under one roof.

ANTIQUE PARADISE
5828 Sunset Drive
South Miami, Fla. 33143
(305) 666-1135
Clocks, china, glass, and oak furniture.

ANTIQUE WICKER
2921 SW 72nd Street
Miami, Fla. 33143
(305) 264-9996
Victorian, turn-of-the-century, and Art Deco wicker and rattan.

FRANCES CARY ANTIQUES
11077 Biscayne Boulevard
Miami, Fla. 33161
(305) 891-6196
Specializing in Art Deco and art moderne.

LAST TANGO IN PARIS
422 Espanola Way
Miami Beach, Fla. 33139
(305) 532-4228
Vintage and Art Deco collectibles.

MIAMI TWICE
6576 SW 40th Street
Miami, Fla. 33145
(305) 666-0127
Vintage clothing, jewelry, furniture, and collectibles.

MORGANSTERN'S ANTIQUES
2665 Coral Way
Miami, Fla. 33145
(305) 854-2744
Modern Latin American and Cuban art, old oriental rugs, tapestries, paintings and prints, furniture, pottery, and porcelain.

NAUTICAL LOFT
5805 Sunset Drive
South Miami, Fla. 33143
(305) 665-9661
Marine antiques, clocks, telescopes, sextants, books, maps.

NED'S ANTIQUES
7328 Red Road
South Miami, Fla. 33143
(305) 667-3538
Art Deco, Art Nouveau, lamps, Tiffany; expert restoration work.

ROSE'S ANTIQUES AND GIFTS
6350 SW 40th Street
Miami, Fla. 33155
(305) 667-8703
Collectibles, furniture, glass, and china.

VALERIO ANTIQUES
3390 Mary Street
Coconut Grove, Fla. 33133
(305) 448-6779
Art Nouveau and Art Deco.

Artists

Each of these artists, whose work is featured in some of the Miami homes here, has a distinctive style, often with a tropical flair that can be seen nowhere else in the country.

SILVIA ACOSTA
1721 SW 126th Place
Miami, Fla. 33175
(305) 551-7846

DALE BEATTY
2815 Bayview Drive
Naples, Fla. 33962
(813) 775-5113

CRAIG BIONDI
5291 Alton Road
Miami Beach, Fla. 33140
(305) 864-4084

THE SKULL SISTERS
1444 Pennsylvania Avenue
Miami Beach, Fla. 33139
(305) 672-3435

CANDACE WALTERS
370 South Main Street
Mansfield, Mass. 02048
(617) 339-5608

JEAN WELCH
116 Tangelo Court
Maitland, Fla. 32751
(407) 645-0579

DEBRA LYNN YATES
7291 SW 52nd Court
South Miami, Fla. 33143
(305) 666-6180

Art Galleries Specializing in Florida and Caribbean Artists

THE ART PLACE AT
CAULEY SQUARE
22400 Old Dixie Highway
Miami, Fla. 33189
(305) 258-4222

BACARDI ART GALLERY
2100 Biscayne Boulevard
Miami, Fla. 33137
(305) 573-8511

BARBARA GILLMAN GALLERY
270 NE 39th Street
Miami, Fla. 33137
(305) 573-4898

BARBARA GILLMAN GALLERY
3105 Bay to Bay Boulevard
Tampa, Fla. 33629
(813) 831-9987

BARBARA GREENE GALLERY
4200 Aurora Street
Coconut Grove, Fla. 33133
(305) 448-9229

GALERIE HELENE GRUBAIR
7188 SW 47th Street
Miami, Fla. 33165
(305) 666-4354

GLORIA LURIA GALLERY
1033 Kane Concourse
Bay Harbor Island,
Fla. 33154
(305) 865-3060

MORGANSTERN'S LATIN
AMERICAN & CUBAN ART
2665 Coral Way
Miami, Fla. 33129
(305) 884-2744

THIS SIDE OF THE CARIBBEAN
910 Lincoln Road
Miami Beach, Fla. 33139
(305) 532-9776

Architects

CARL ABBOTT, FAIA
2846 Riverside Drive
Sarasota, Fla. 34234
(813) 351-5016

ARQUITECTONICA
2151 Le Jeune Road,
Suite 300
Coral Gables, Fla. 33134
(305) 442-9381

THOMAS COPPAGE,
ARCHITECTURAL DESIGNER
904 Milan Avenue
Coral Gables, Fla. 33134
(305) 448-0962 and 446-6877

ANDRES DUANY/ELIZABETH
PLATER-ZYBERK,
ARCHITECTS, AIA
2949 Coconut Avenue
Miami, Fla. 33133
(305) 445-7602

ALEX GORLIN, AIA
155 West 91st Street
New York, N.Y. 10024
(212) 496-8580

MARK HAMPTON, AIA
3900 Loquat Avenue
Coconut Grove, Fla. 33133
(305) 443-6946

OSWALD LEAL,
ARCHITECTURAL DESIGNER
904 Milan Avenue
Coral Cables, Fla. 33134
(305) 448-0962 and 446-6877

Juan Lezcano, RA
1214 SW 12th Court
Miami, Fla. 33135
(305) 856-5239

Suzanne Martinson, AIA
7910 SW 54th Court
South Miami, Fla. 33143
(305) 667-3944

Michael Steffans, RA
832 Santiago Street
Coral Gables, Fla. 33134
(305) 444-0528

Alex Sturman, RA
10500 SW 108th Avenue,
#B-414
Miami, Fla. 33176
(305) 279-2313

Daniel Williams, AIA
2424 South Dixie Highway,
Suite 200
Miami, Fla. 33133
(305) 858-4144

Beach and Garden Umbrellas

Beach-o-rama
2017 Wilson Street
Hollywood, Fla. 33020
(305) 945-0695

Weather or Not
5703 South Travelers
Palm Lane
Tamarac, Fla. 33319
(305) 940-1490

Weather or Not
Aventura Mall
Ft. Lauderdale, Fla. 33301
(305) 935-5240

Chickees

The thatched huts of Indians native to southern Florida are still used as ornamental garden structures. Miccosukee craftsmen will erect chickees on site.

Chickee Craftsman Pete Osceola
18799 SW 8th Street
Miami, Fla. 33199
(305) 223-5055

Miccosukee Indian Chickee Huts
18799 SW 8th Street
Miami, Fla. 33199
(305) 559-2849

Furniture Showrooms

Antares
2640 SW 28th Lane
Miami, Fla. 33133
(305) 854-1211
Interpretive contemporary furniture.

Decolectables
233 14th Street
Miami Beach, Fla. 33139
(305) 674-0899
Art Deco, 1940s and 1950s furniture and collectibles.

Knoll International
4200 Aurora Street
Coral Gables, Fla. 33134
(305) 446-0211
Classic modern furniture.

LUMINAIRE
2331 Ponce de Leon
Boulevard
Coral Gables, Fla. 33146
(305) 448-7367
*Italian and Scandinavian
contemporary residential
and office furniture and
accessories.*

SOUTH BEACH FURNITURE
COMPANY
121 5th Street
Miami Beach, Fla. 33139
(305) 532-2997
*Specializing in refinished
Art Deco, 1940s and 1950s
furniture, custom
refinishing, and
reupholstery.*

Fruit Stands
and Shippers

ATHENS TROPICAL FRUITS
AND NOVELTIES
6976 Collins Avenue
Miami Beach, Fla. 33141
(305) 865-9119

DEW PROCESS
17671 133 Way
North Jupiter, Fla. 33478
(407) 744-1515
*Easy-crack coconuts,
alfalfa, and variety bean
sprouts.*

FERRIS GROVES
530 Arthur Godfrey Road
Miami Beach, Fla. 33141
(305) 530-0350
*Bonded fruit shippers:
avocadoes, limes,
pineapple, oranges,
grapefruit, and mangoes.*

LEFRAN CORPORATION
7875 NW 12th Street
Miami, Fla. 33172
(305) 592-3658
Exotic Caribbean produce.

NORMAN BROTHERS PRODUCE
7621 SW 87th Avenue
Miami, Fla. 33176
(305) 274-9363
*Fruits, vegetables, fresh
herbs, and fresh-squeezed
juices.*

RARE FRUIT COUNCIL
INTERNATIONAL
13609 Old Cutler Road
Miami, Fla. 33170
(305) 238-1360

TODD'S FRUIT SHIPPERS
221 Navarre Avenue
Coral Gables, Fla. 33134
(305) 448-5215
Tropical candies and jellies.

WRAP AND PACK
9808 South Dixie Highway
Miami, Fla. 33156
(305) 661-6331
*Gourmet and fruit gift
baskets, stone crabs, and
lobsters.*

Garden
Centers

BOTANICAL GARDEN CENTER
19110 Krome Avenue
Miami, Fla. 33187
(305) 235-0118

NATURELAND GARDEN
CENTERS
17171 South Dixie Highway
Miami, Fla. 33157
(305) 235-0118

NATURELAND GARDEN
CENTERS
8523 South Dixie Highway
Miami, Fla. 33156
(305) 665-3673

Garden
Ornaments

DENMARK'S ART STONE
12351 NW 7th Avenue
Miami, Fla. 33150
(305) 681-6641

Interior Designers

MARJORIE GOLDMAN, ASID
832 Santiago Street
Coral Gables, Fla. 33134
(305) 444-0528

DENNIS JENKINS, ASID
5815 SW 68th Street
South Miami, Fla. 33143
(305) 662-2166

DALE MONTGOMERY, ASID
McMillen Inc.
155 East 56th Street
New York, N.Y. 10022
(212) 753-5600

Landscape Architects

LEONARDO ALVAREZ, ASLA
Leonardo Alvarez &
Associates
4950 SW 72nd Avenue
Suite 104
Miami, Fla. 33155
(305) 667-3534

RAYMOND JUNGLES, ASLA
7291 SW 52nd Court
South Miami, Fla. 33143
(305) 666-9299

Orchid Growers

FABULOUS GARDENS
9550 SW 67th Avenue
Miami, Fla. 33156
(305) 661-1217

ROBERT FUCHS ORCHIDS
28100 SW 182nd Avenue
Homestead, Fla. 33189
(305) 245-4570

JONES & SCULLY
18955 SW 168th Street
Miami, Fla. 33157
(305) 238-7000

ORCHID WORLD
INTERNATIONAL
10885 SW 95th Street
Miami, Fla. 33176
(305) 271-0268

Public Houses, Gardens, and Collections

AUDUBON HOUSE
AND GARDENS
205 Whitehead Street
Key West, Fla. 33040
(305) 294-2116
*Restored 19th-century home
of Capt. John H. Geiger
with displays of Audubon
engravings.*

THE BARNACLE
3485 Main Highway
Coconut Grove, Fla.
33233-0995
(305) 448-9445
*Home of Commodore Ralph
Munroe, built in 1891.*

PRESTON BIRD AND
MARY HEINLEIN FRUIT
AND SPICE PARK
24801 SW 187th Avenue
Miami, Fla. 33170
(305) 247-5727
*More than 700 varieties of
fruits, nuts, herbs, and
vegetables.*

BONNET HOUSE
900 North Birch Road
Ft. Lauderdale, Fla. 33304
(305) 563-5393
*The tropical plantation–
style winter estate of artists
Frederick and Evelyn
Bartlett on 35 acres.*

CORAL GABLES HOUSE
907 Coral Way
Coral Gables, Fla. 33134
(305) 442-6593
*Pioneer developer George
Merrick's family home, built
in 1898.*

THOMAS A. EDISON
WINTER HOME
2350 McGregor Boulevard
Ft. Myers, Fla. 33901
(305) 334-3614
*Winter home and workshop
of the famous inventor.*

FAIRCHILD TROPICAL GARDEN
10901 Old Cutler Road
Miami, Fla. 33170
(305) 667-1651
*One of the finest and most
varied botanical gardens in
the world.*

FLAMINGO GARDENS
3750 Flamingo Road
Ft. Lauderdale, Fla. 33330
(305) 473-0010
Sixty acres of tropical and botanical gardens, plus a 200-year-old live oak and petting zoo.

HEMINGWAY HOUSE
907 Whitehead Street
Key West, Fla. 33040
(305) 294-1575
The Southern residence of Ernest Hemingway, built in 1851.

KING CROMARTI HOUSE
Discovery Center
231 SW 2nd Avenue
Ft. Lauderdale, Fla. 33301
(305) 462-4115
House built in 1907 by Edwin Thomas King with turn-of-the century furniture, artifacts.

MORIKAMI MUSEUM GARDEN
4000 Morikami Park Road
Delray Beach, Fla. 33446
(305) 495-0233
Formal Japanese public garden.

MOUNTS HORTICULTURAL BOTANICAL GARDEN
North of Southern Boulevard on Military Trail
West Palm Beach, Fla. 33415-1395
(407) 233-1700
Extensive tropical, subtropical plants, fern house, and rain forest.

ORCHID JUNGLE
26715 SW 157th Avenue
Homestead, Fla. 33023
(305) 247-4824

PARROT JUNGLE
11000 SW 57th Avenue
(Red Road)
Miami, Fla. 33156
(305) 666-7834
Exotic bird attraction and very exotic botanical garden.

SPANISH MONASTERY AND FORMAL GARDENS
16711 West Dixie Highway
Miami, Fla. 33160
(305) 945-1462
800-year-old monastery shipped from Spain and reassembled here.

STRANAHAN HOUSE
One Stranahan Place
Ft. Lauderdale, Fla. 33301
(305) 463-4374
Restored home of Ft. Lauderdale pioneers Frank and Ivy Stranahan, built in 1901.

VIZCAYA
3251 South Miami Avenue
Miami, Fla. 33129
(305) 579-2318
Italian Renaissance–style villa and formal gardens.

WHITEHALL
One Cocoanut Row and Whitehall Way
Palm Beach, Fla. 33480
(407) 655-2833
The Henry Flagler mansion, built in 1901.

THE MITCHELL WOLFSON, JR., COLLECTION OF DECORATIVE AND PROPAGANDA ARTS
Miami-Dade Community College
New World Campus
300 NE 2nd Avenue,
3rd Floor
Miami, Fla. 33132
(305) 347-3042
Late 19th- and early 20th-century work.

WRECKER'S MUSEUM
322 Duval Street
Key West, Fla. 33140
(305) 294-9502

Publications and Programs

Florida Home & Garden Magazine
600 Brickell Avenue
Miami, Fla. 33131
(305) 374-5011

The Miami Herald
1 Herald Plaza
Miami, Fla. 33131
(305) 350-2111

The Wave
7752 NW 54th Street
Miami, Fla. 33166
(305) 594-7323

THE ENVIRONMENTAL CENTER
Miami Dade Community College
11011 SW 104th Street
Miami, Fla. 33176
(305) 596-4113
Courses in home building, gardening, and cooking.

Rattan and Wicker

EMPIRE RATTAN
3300 NW 79th Avenue
Miami, Fla. 33155
(305) 592-2056

MR. RATTAN
11381 West Flagler Street
Miami, Fla. 33174
(305) 559-4928

PIER 1 IMPORTS
1630 NE 164th Street
North Miami Beach, Fla. 33162
(305) 944-5042

PIER 1 IMPORTS
1224 South Dixie Highway
Coral Gables, Fla. 33146
(305) 665-6566

PIER 1 IMPORTS
14104 South Dixie Highway
Miami, Fla. 33176
(305) 251-6212

WICKER WAREHOUSE
5280 NW 77th Court
Miami, Fla. 33166
(305) 593-0919

Shells

ALMARK CORAL AND SHELLS
76 NW 72nd Street
Miami, Fla. 33150
(305) 756-0431

ART BY GOD
7123 SW 117th Avenue
Miami, Fla. 33183
(305) 274-4044

ATLANTIC CORAL ENTERPRISE
2280 SW 66th Terrace
Ft. Lauderdale, Fla. 33317
(305) 475-9040

CARIBBEAN ADVENTURES
6903 NW 42nd Street
Miami, Fla. 33155
(305) 591-4118

Terrazzo

AMERICAN TERRAZZO AND TILE
1915 NW Miami Court
Miami, Fla. 33136
(305) 573-6464

Tile and Terra Cotta

ARCHITECTURAL MARBLE IMPORTERS, INC.
1166 Snead Avenue
Sarasota, Fla. 34237
(813) 365-3552

CERAMICA, INC.
949 U.S. Highway 19 South
Palm Harbor, Fla. 34684
(813) 784-1865

CERAMICA, INC.
7713 Anderson Road
Tampa, Fla. 33632
(813) 886-7535

CLASSIC TILE & BATH
3620 Silver Star Road
Orlando, Fla. 32804
(407) 299-1251

COUNTRY FLOORS
94 NE 40th Street
Miami, Fla. 33137
(305) 576-0421

COUNTRY FLOORS
15 East 16th Street
New York, N.Y. 10003
(212) 627-8300

COUNTRY FLOORS
8735 Melrose Avenue
Los Angeles, Calif. 90069
(213) 657-0510

COUNTRY FLOORS
1706 Locust Street
Philadelphia, Pa. 19103
(215) 545-1040

COUNTRY FLOORS
Dunan Materials
1095 SE 9th Terrace
Hialeah, Fla. 33010
(305) 888-6443

FORMS AND SURFACES
3801 NE 2nd Avenue
Miami, Fla. 33137
(305) 576-1880
(1-800) 432-2048

IBERIA TILES
4221 Ponce de Leon
Boulevard
Coral Gables, Fla. 33134
(305) 446-0222

MEXI-FLOORS
14371 SW 119th Avenue
Miami, Fla. 33186
(305) 233-8745

PAN AMERICAN MARBLE
& STONE CO.
6825 NW 25th Street
Miami, Fla. 33152
(305) 887-3090

SANTA ROSA MARBLE
3400 NW 77th Court
Miami, Fla. 33122
(305) 591-3744

SANTA ROSA MARBLE
305 West 21st Street
Hialeah, Fla. 33010
(305) 887-0355

SUNNY MCLEAN & COMPANY
3800 NE 2nd Avenue
Miami, Fla. 33137
(305) 573-5943

SYKES TILE
1601 NW 82nd Avenue
Miami, Fla. 33126
(305) 591-0012

SYKES TILE
3484 NE 12th Avenue
Ft. Lauderdale, Fla. 33334
(305) 563-5666

SYKES TILE
425 Belvedere Road
West Palm Beach, Fla.
33405
(305) 833-5727

SYKES TILE
791 SE Monterey Road
Stuart, Fla. 34994
(305) 283-1362

TAMIAMI TILE
7500 NW 41st Street
Miami, Fla. 33166
(305) 592-2600

TILE COUNCIL OF AMERICA
PO Box 326
Princeton, N.J. 08542-0326
(609) 921-7050

TROPICAL CUBAN TILE
COMPANY
3632 NW 37th Avenue
Miami, Fla. 33142
(305) 633-8941

Tours and Attractions

ART DECO DISTRICT TOURS
1236 Ocean Drive
Miami Beach, Fla. 33139
(305) 672-2014

BISCAYNE NATIONAL PARK
TOUR BOATS
Biscayne National Park
Headquarters
Homestead, Fla. 33033
(305) 375-0486
*Architecture, history, and
colorful landmarks tours
given by the Miami Design
Preservation League.*

CORAL CASTLE
28655 South Federal
Highway
Homestead, Fla. 33033
(305) 248-6344
*Claimed to be the eighth
wonder of the world.*

EVERGLADES MICCOSUKEE
INDIAN VILLAGE AND
AIRBOAT RIDES
Miccosoukee Reservation,
U.S. Highway 41
(25 miles west of Miami on
SW 8th Street)
(305) 223-8380
*Indian museum, alligator
wrestling, crafts exhibits,
gifts shop, and restaurant.*

EVERGLADES SAFARI PARK
26700 SW 8th Street
Miami, Fla. 33199
(15 miles west of the
turnpike on the Tamiami
Trail)
(305) 226-6923
*Guided air boat tours,
alligator farm, nature trail,
and Indian village.*

HISTORICAL MUSEUM OF
SOUTHERN FLORIDA
101 West Flagler Street
Miami, Fla. 33131
(305) 375-1492

ISLAND QUEEN
400 SE 2nd Avenue
Miami, Fla. 33131
(305) 379-5119
*Boat tour of sites and stars'
homes around Biscayne
Bay.*

MIAMI SEAQUARIUM
Rickenbacker Causeway
Key Biscayne, Fla. 33149
(305) 361-5703
*Whales, dolphins, and
tropical fish.*

MUSEUM OF SCIENCE AND
PLANETARIUM
3280 South Miami Avenue
Miami, Fla. 33129
(305) 854-2222

PLANET OCEAN
3979 Rickenbacker
Causeway
Key Biscayne, Fla. 33149
(305) 361-9455
*Ocean science museum with
hands-on exhibits and
special effects.*

SKYRIDER OF MIAMI
Miamarina at Bayside
Miami, Fla. 33131
(305) 374-4448
*A view of the Miami skyline
from a flotation chair in the
sky pulled by a luxury motor
boat.*

index